Modern Critical Interpretations

George Orwell's
1984

Modern Critical Interpretations

These and other titles in preparation

Modern Critical Interpretations

George Orwell's
1984

Edited and with an introduction by

Harold Bloom
Sterling Professor of the Humanities
Yale University

Chelsea House Publishers ◊ *1987*

NEW YORK ◊ NEW HAVEN ◊ PHILADELPHIA

© 1987 by Chelsea House Publishers, a division
of Chelsea House Educational Communications, Inc.
  133 Christopher Street, New York, NY 10014
  345 Whitney Avenue, New Haven, CT 06511
  5014 West Chester Pike, Edgemont, PA 19028

Introduction © 1987 by Harold Bloom

Printed and bound in the United States of America

∞ The paper used in this publication meets the minimum requirements
of the American National Standard for Permanence of Paper for Printed
Library Materials, Z39.48-1984.

Library of Congress Cataloging-in-Publication Data
George Orwell's Nineteen eighty-four.

  (Modern critical interpretations)
  Bibliography: p.
  Includes index.
  1. Orwell, George, 1903–1950. Nineteen eighty-four.
I. Bloom, Harold.   II. Series.
PR6029.R8N4944   1987   823'.912   86–21577
ISBN 1–55546–026–7

Contents

Editor's Note

This volume collects a representative selection of what I judge to be the most useful criticism of George Orwell's most widely read fiction, *1984*. I am grateful to Peter Childers for his devotion and skill in helping me to edit this book.

The essays included here are arranged in the chronological order of their original publication. My introduction severely doubts whether *1984* can survive as more than a virtuous period piece, curiously akin to Stowe's *Uncle Tom's Cabin* and other "good bad books."

Raymond Williams begins the chronological sequence by questioning the general validity of Orwell's political conclusions while valuing his honest and compassionate observation of the intellectual as an exile or victim within society. A rather surprising reading of *1984* as a Freudian work, by Paul Roazen, emphasizes how both Orwell and Freud heighten our perceptual awareness of reality by subjecting reality to a disproportionate mode of representation.

The novelist Anthony Burgess, writing with his customary gusto, analyzes the metaphysics of Orwell's Oceania as subtly solipsistic, and so judges *1984* to be not only "a Swiftian toy" but also "an extended metaphor of apprehension." In a feminist critique, Daphne Patai both condemns Orwell for his conventional misogyny and praises him for his despair, since supposedly that ensued from his awareness of the deadly potential of his dangerous notion of masculinity.

In a strong attack upon Orwell's acute limitations as a theorist of language, Roy Harris condemns Newspeak as a misleading figment of a false linguistics. Irving Howe, very much at variance with the editor's introduction, returns to *1984* and finds it to be one of the authentic literary classics of our time. Whether Howe is not confusing the aesthetic and the moral realms may not be altogether clear, but he is eloquent in support of his judgment. Finally, Vita Fortunati examines *1984* against the literary tradition of utopias and provides us with a dialectical reading of the narrative.

Introduction

I

There is an equivocal irony to reading, and writing about, George Orwell in 1986. I have just reread *1984*, *Animal Farm*, and many of the essays for the first time in some years, and I find myself lost in an interplay of many contending reactions, moral and aesthetic. Orwell, aesthetically considered, is a far better essayist than novelist. Lionel Trilling, reviewing *1984* in 1984, praised the book, with a singular moral authority:

> The whole effort of the culture of the last hundred years has been directed toward teaching us to understand the economic motive as the irrational road to death, and to seek salvation in the rational and the planned. Orwell marks a turn in thought; he asks us to consider whether the triumph of certain forces of the mind, in their naked pride and excess, may not produce a state of things far worse than any we have ever known. He is not the first to raise the question, but he is the first to raise it on truly liberal or radical grounds, with no intention of abating the demand for a just society, and with an overwhelming intensity and passion. This priority makes his book a momentous one.

The book remains momentous; perhaps it always will be so. But there is nothing intrinsic to the book that will determine its future importance. Its very genre will be established by political, social, economic events. Is it satire or science fiction or dystopia or counter-manifesto? Last week I read newspaper accounts of two recent speeches, perorations delivered by President Reagan and by Norman Podhoretz, each favorably citing Orwell. The President, awarding medals to Senator Barry Goldwater and Helen Hayes, among others, saw them as exemplars of Orwell's belief in freedom and individual dignity, while the sage Podhoretz allowed himself to observe that Orwell would have become a neoconservative had he but survived until this moment. Perhaps irony, however equivocal, is inadequate to represent so curious a posthumous fate as has come to the author of *Homage to Catalonia*, a man who went to Barcelona to fight for the Party of Marxist Unity and the Anarcho-Syndicalists.

V. S. Prichett and others were correct in describing Orwell as the best of modern pamphleteers. A pamphlet certainly can achieve aesthetic eminence; "tracts and pamphlets" is a major genre, particularly in Great Britain, where its masters include Milton, Defoe, Swift, Dr. Johnson, Burke, Blake, Shelley, Carlyle, Ruskin, and Newman. Despite his celebrated mastery of the plain style, it is rather uncertain that Orwell has joined himself to that company. I suspect that he is closer to the category that he once described as "good bad books," giving Harriet Beecher Stowe's *Uncle Tom's Cabin* as a supreme instance. Aesthetically considered, *1984* is very much the *Uncle Tom's Cabin* of our time, with poor Winston Smith as Uncle Tom, the unhappy Julia as little Eva, and the more-than-sadistic O'Brien as Simon Legree. I do not find O'Brien to be as memorable as Simon Legree, but then that is part of Orwell's point. We have moved into a world in which our torturers also have suffered a significant loss of personality.

II

Orwell's success as a prophet is necessarily a mixed one, since his relative crudity as a creator of character obliges us to read *1984* rather literally. What works best in the novel is its contextualization of all the phrases it has bequeathed to our contemporary language, though whether to *the* language is not yet certain. Newspeak and doublethink, "War Is Peace," "Freedom Is Slavery," "Ignorance Is Strength," "Big Brother Is Watching You," the Thought Police, the Two Minutes Hate, the Ministry of Truth, and all the other Orwellian inventions that are now wearisome clichés, are restored to some force, though little freshness, when we encounter them where they first arose.

Unfortunately, in itself that does not suffice. Even a prophetic pamphlet requires eloquence, if we are to return to it and find ourselves affected at least as much as we were before. *1984* can hurt you a single time, and most likely when you are young. After that, defensive laughter becomes the aesthetic problem. Rereading *1984* can be too much like watching a really persuasive horror movie; humor acquires the validity of health. Contemporary reviewers, even Trilling, were too overwhelmed by the book's relevance to apprehend its plain badness as narrative or Orwell's total inability to represent even a curtailed human personality or moral character.

Mark Schorer's response in the *New York Times Book Review* may have seemed appropriate on June 12, 1949, but its hyperboles now provoke polite puzzlement:

> No real reader can neglect this experience with impunity. He will be moved by Smith's wistful attempts to remember a different kind of life from his. He will make a whole new discovery of the beauty of love between man and woman, and of the strange beauty of landscape in a totally mechanized world. He will be asked to read through pages of sustained physical and psychological pain that have seldom been equaled and never in such quiet, sober prose. And he will return to his own life from Smith's escape into living death with a resolution to resist power wherever it means to deny him his individuality, and to resist for himself the poisonous lures of power.

Would it make a difference now if Orwell had given his book the title *1994*? Our edge of foreboding has vanished when we contemplate the book, if indeed we ought to regard it as a failed apocalypse. Yet all apocalypses, in the literary sense, are failed apocalypses, so that if they fade, the phenomenon of literary survival or demise clearly takes precedence over whatever status social prophecy affords. The limits of Orwell's achievement are clarified if we juxtapose it directly to the authentic American apocalypses of our time: Faulkner's *As I Lay Dying*, Nathanael West's *Miss Lonelyhearts*, Thomas Pynchon's *Gravity's Rainbow*. Why do they go on wounding us, reading after reading, while *1984* threatens to become a period piece, however nightmarish? It would be absurdly unfair to look at *1984* side by side with Kafka and Beckett; Orwell was in no way an aspirant after the sublime, however demonic or diminished. But he was a satirist, and in *1984* a kind of phantasmagoric realist. If his O'Brien is not of the stature of the unamiable Simon Legree, he is altogether nonexistent as a satanic rhetorician if we attempt to bring him into the company of West's Shrike.

Can a novel survive praise that endlessly centers upon its author's humane disposition, his indubitable idealism, his personal honesty, his political courage, his moral nature? Orwell may well have been the exemplary and representative socialist intellectual of our time (though Raymond Williams, the crucial Marxist literary critic in Great Britain, definitely does not think so). But very bad men and women have written superb novels, and great moralists have written unreadable ones. *1984* is neither superb nor unreadable. If it resembles the work of a precursor figure, that figure is surely H. G. Wells, as Wyndham Lewis shrewdly realized. Wells surpasses Orwell in storytelling vigor, in pungency of characterization, and in imaginative invention, yet Wells now seems remote and Orwell remains very close. We are driven back to what makes *1984* a good bad book: relevance. The book substitutes for a real and universal fear: that in the political and economic area, the dreadful is still about to happen. Yet the book again lacks a defense against its own blunderings into the ridiculous. As social prophecy, it is closer to Sinclair Lewis's now forgotten *It Can't Happen Here* than to Nathanael West's still hilarious *A Cool Million*, where Big Brother, under the name of Shagpoke Whipple, speaks uncannily in the accents shared by Calvin Coolidge and Ronald Reagan. Why could not Orwell have rescued his book by some last touch of irony or by a valid invocation of the satiric Muse?

III

What Max Horkheimer and T. W. Adorno grimly called the Culture Industry has absorbed Orwell, and his *1984* in particular. Is this because Orwell retains such sentimentalities or soft idealisms as the poignance of true love? After all, Winston and Julia are terrorized out of love by brute pain and unendurable fear; no one could regard them as having been culpable in their forced abandonment of one another. This is akin to Orwell's fantastic and wholly unconvincing hope that the proles might yet offer salvation, a hope presumably founded upon the odd notion that Oceania lets eighty-five percent of its population go back to nature in the slums of London and other cities. Love and the working class are therefore pretty much undamaged in Orwell's vision. Contrast Pynchon's imaginative "paranoia" in *Gravity's Rainbow*, where all of us, of whatever social class, live in the Zone which is dominated by the truly paranoid System, and where authentic love can be represented only as sadomasochism. There is a Counterforce in *Gravity's Rainbow* that fights the System, but it is ineffectual, farcical, and can be animated only by the peculiar ideology that Pynchon calls sado-anarchism, an ideology that the Culture Industry cannot absorb, and that I suspect Adorno gladly would have embraced.

I don't intend this introduction as a drubbing or trashing of Orwell and *1984*, and *Gravity's Rainbow*, being an encyclopedic prose epic, is hardly a fair agonist against which *1984* should be matched. But the aesthetic badness of *1984* is palpable enough, and I am a good enough disciple of the divine Oscar Wilde to wonder if an aesthetic inadequacy really can be a moral splendor. Simon Legree beats poor old Uncle Tom to death, and O'Brien pretty well wrecks Winston Smith's body and then reduces him to supposed ruin by threatening him with some particularly nasty and hungry rats. Is

Uncle Tom's Cabin actually a moral achievement, even if Harriet Beecher Stowe hastened both the Civil War and the Emancipation Proclamation? Is *1984* a moral triumph, even if it hastens a multiplication of neoconservatives?

The defense of a literary period piece cannot differ much from a defense of period pieces in clothes, household objects, popular music, movies, and the lower reaches of the visual arts. A period piece that is a political and social polemic, like *Uncle Tom's Cabin* and *1984*, acquires a curious charm of its own. What partly saves *1984* from Orwell's overliteralness and failures in irony is the strange archaism of its psychology and rhetoric:

> He paused for a few moments, as though to allow what he had been saying to sink in.
>
> "Do you remember," he went on, "writing in your diary, 'Freedom is the freedom to say that two plus two make four'?"
>
> "Yes," said Winston.
>
> O'Brien held up his left hand, its back toward Winston, with the thumb hidden and the four fingers extended.
>
> "How many fingers am I holding up, Winston?"
>
> "Four."
>
> "And if the Party says that it is not four but five — then how many?"
>
> "Four."
>
> The word ended in a gasp of pain. The needle of the dial had shot up to fifty-five. The sweat had sprung out all over Winston's body. The air tore into his lungs and issued again in deep groans which even by clenching his teeth he could not stop. O'Brien watched him, the four fingers still extended. He drew back the lever. This time the pain was only slightly eased.
>
> "How many fingers, Winston?"
>
> "Four."
>
> The needle went up to sixty.
>
> "How many fingers, Winston?"
>
> "Four! Four! What else can I say? Four!"
>
> The needle must have risen again, but he did not look at it. The heavy, stern face and the four fingers filled his vision. The fingers stood up before his eyes like pillars, enormous, blurry, and seeming to vibrate, but unmistakably four.
>
> "How many fingers, Winston?"
>
> "Four! Stop it, stop it! How can you go on? Four! Four!"
>
> "How many fingers, Winston?"

"Five! Five! Five!"

"No, Winston, that is no use. You are lying. You still think there are four. How many fingers, please?"

"Four! Five! Four! Anything you like. Only stop it, stop the pain!"

Abruptly he was sitting up with O'Brien's arm round his shoulders. He had perhaps lost consciousness for a few seconds. The bonds that had held his body down were loosened. He felt very cold, he was shaking uncontrollably, his teeth were chattering, the tears were rolling down his cheeks. For a moment he clung to O'Brien like a baby, curiously comforted by the heavy arm round his shoulders. He had the feeling that O'Brien was his protector, that the pain was something that came from outside, from some other source, and that it was O'Brien who would save him from it.

"You are a slow learner, Winston," said O'Brien gently.

"How can I help it?" he blubbered. "How can I help seeing what is in front of my eyes? Two and two are four."

"Sometimes, Winston. Sometimes they are five. Sometimes they are three. Sometimes they are all of them at once. You must try harder. It is not easy to become sane."

He laid Winston down on the bed. The grip on his limbs tightened again, but the pain had ebbed away and the trembling had stopped, leaving him merely weak and cold. O'Brien motioned with his head to the man in the white coat, who had stood immobile throughout the proceedings. The man in the white coat bent down and looked closely into Winston's eyes, felt his pulse, laid an ear against his chest, tapped here and there; then he nodded to O'Brien.

"Again," said O'Brien.

The pain flowed into Winston's body. The needle must be at seventy, seventy-five. He had shut his eyes this time. He knew that the fingers were still there, and still four. All that mattered was somehow to stay alive until the spasm was over. He had ceased to notice whether he was crying out or not. The pain lessened again. He opened his eyes. O'Brien had drawn back the lever.

"How many fingers, Winston?"

"Four. I suppose there are four. I would see five if I could. I am trying to see five."

"Which do you wish: to persuade me that you see five, or really to see them?"

"Really to see them."

"Again," said O'Brien.

If we took this with high seriousness, then its offense against any persuasive mode of representation would make us uneasy. But it *is* a grand period piece, parodying not only Stalin's famous trials, but many theologically inspired ordeals before the advent of the belated Christian heresy that Russian Marxism actually constitutes. Orwell was a passionate moralist, and an accomplished essayist. The age drove him to the composition of political romance, though he lacked nearly all of the gifts necessary for the writer of narrative fiction. *1984* is an honorable aesthetic failure, and perhaps time will render its crudities into so many odd period graces, remnants of a vanished era. Yet the imagination, as Wallace Stevens once wrote, is always at the end of an era. Lionel Trilling thought that O'Brien's torture of Winston Smith was "a hideous parody on psychotherapy and the Platonic dialogues." Thirty-seven years after Trilling's review, the scene I have quoted above seems more like self-parody, as though Orwell's narrative desperately sought its own reduction, its own outrageous descent into the fallacy of believing that only the worst truth about us can be the truth.

Orwell was a dying man as he wrote the book, suffering the wasting away of his body in consumption. D. H. Lawrence, dying the same way, remained a heroic vitalist, as his last poems and stories demonstrate. But Lawrence belonged to literary culture, to the old, high line of transcendental seers. What wanes and dies in *1984* is not the best of George Orwell, not the pamphleteer of *The Lion and the Unicorn* nor the autobiographer of *Homage to Catalonia* nor the essayist of "Shooting an Elephant." That Orwell lived and died an independent socialist, hardly Marxist but really a Spanish anarchist or an English dissenter and rebel, of the line of Cromwell and of Cromwell's celebrators, Milton and Carlyle. *1984* has the singular power, not aesthetic but social, of being the product of an age, and not just of the man who set it down.

George Orwell

Raymond Williams

"It is not so much a series of books, it is more like a world." This is Orwell, on Dickens. "It is not so much a series of books, it is more like a case." This, today, is Orwell himself. We have been using him, since his death, as the ground for a general argument, but this is not mainly an argument about ideas, it is an argument about mood. It is not that he was a great artist, whose experience we have slowly to receive and value. It is not that he was an important thinker, whose ideas we have to interpret and examine. His interest lies almost wholly in his frankness. With us, he inherited a great and humane tradition; with us, he sought to apply it to the contemporary world. He went to books, and found in them the detail of virtue and truth. He went to experience, and found in it the practice of loyalty, tolerance and sympathy. But, in the end,

> it was a bright cold day in April, and the clocks were striking thirteen. Winston Smith, his chin nuzzled into his breast in an effort to escape the vile wind, slipped quickly through the glass doors of Victory Mansions, though not quickly enough to prevent a swirl of gritty dust from entering along with him.

The dust is part of the case: the caustic dust carried by the vile wind. Democracy, truth, art, equality, culture: all these we carry in our heads, but, in the street, the wind is everywhere. The great and humane tradition is a

---

From *Culture and Society 1780–1950*. ©1958 by Raymond Williams. Columbia University Press, 1958.

kind of wry joke; in the books it served, but put them down and look around you. It is not so much a disillusion, it is more like our actual world.

The situation is paradox: this kind of tradition, this kind of dust. We have made Orwell the figure of this paradox: in reacting to him we are reacting to a common situation. England took the first shock of industrialism and its consequences, and from this it followed, on the one hand, that the humane response was early, fine and deep—the making of a real tradition; on the other hand that the material constitution of what was criticized was built widely into all our lives—a powerful and committed reality. The interaction has been long, slow and at times desperate. A man who lives it on his own senses is subject to extraordinary pressures. Orwell lived it, and frankly recorded it: this is why we attend to him. At the same time, although the situation is common, Orwell's response was his own, and has to be distinguished. Neither his affiliations, his difficulties nor his disillusion need to be taken as prescriptive. In the end, for any proper understanding, it is not so much a case, it is a series of books. *refers to "1984"*

The total effect of Orwell's work is an effect of paradox. He was a humane man who communicated an extreme of inhuman terror; a man committed to decency who actualized a distinctive squalor. These, perhaps, are elements of the general paradox. But there are other, more particular, paradoxes. He was a socialist, who popularized a severe and damaging criticism of the idea of socialism and of its adherents. He was a believer in equality, and a critic of class, who founded his later work on a deep assumption of inherent inequality, inescapable class difference. These points have been obscured, or are the subject of merely partisan debate. They can only be approached, adequately, through observation of a further paradox. He was a notable critic of abuse of language, who himself practised certain of its major and typical abuses. He was a fine observer of detail, and appealed as an empiricist, while at the same time committing himself to an unusual amount of plausible yet specious generalization. It is on these points, inherent in the very material of his work, that we must first concentrate.

That he was a fine observer of detail I take for granted; it is the great merit of that group of essays of which *The Art of Donald McGill* is typical, and of parts of *The Road to Wigan Pier*. The contrary observation, on his general judgements, is an effect of the total reading of his work, but some examples may here stand as reminders:

> In each variant of socialism that appeared from about 1900 onwards the aim of establishing liberty and equality was more and more openly abandoned.

The British Labour Party? Guild Socialism?

> By the fourth decade of the twentieth century all the main currents of political thought were authoritarian. The earthly paradise had been discredited at exactly the moment when it became realisable.

England in 1945?

> The first thing that must strike any outside observer is that Socialism in its developed form is a theory confined entirely to the middle class.

A Labour Party conference? Any local party in an industrial constituency? Trade unions?

> All left-wing parties in the highly industrialized countries are at bottom a sham, because they make it their business to fight against something which they do not really wish to destroy.

On what total evidence?

> The energy that actually shapes the world springs from emotions —racial pride, leader worship, religious belief, love of war— which liberal intellectuals mechanically write off as anachronisms, and which they have usually destroyed so completely in themselves as to have lost all power of action.

But does the shaping energy spring from these emotions alone? Is there no other "power of action"?

> A humanitarian is always a hypocrite.

An irritation masquerading as a judgement?

> Take, for instance, the fact that all sensitive people are revolted by industrialism and its products.

All? By all its products?

> I isolate these examples, not only to draw attention to this aspect of Orwell's method, but also to indicate (as all but one of them do) the quality of the disillusion which has, in bulk, been so persuasive. In many of the judgements there is an element of truth, or at least ground for argument, but Orwell's manner is normally to assert, and then to argue within the assertion. As a literary method, the influence of Shaw and Chesterton is clear.

> The method has become that of journalism, and is sometimes praised

as clear forthright statement. Orwell, in his discussions of language, made many very useful points about the language of propaganda. But just as he used plausible assertion, very often, as a means of generalization, so, when he was expressing a prejudice, often of the same basic kind, he moved very easily into the propagandist's kind of emotive abuse:

> One sometimes gets the impression that the mere words "Socialism" and "Communism" draw towards them with magnetic force every fruit-juice drinker, nudist, sandal-wearer, sex-maniac, Quaker, "Nature Cure" quack, pacifist and feminist in England. . . .

> . . . vegetarians with wilting beards . . . shock-headed Marxists chewing polysyllables . . . birth control fanatics and Labour Party backstairs-crawlers.

Or consider his common emotive use of the adjective "little":

> The typical socialist . . . a prim little man with a white-collar job, usually a secret teetotaller and often with vegetarian leanings. . . .

> A rather mean little man, with a white face and a bald head, standing on a platform, shooting out slogans.

> The typical little bowler-hatted sneak—Strube's "little man"—the little docile cit who slips home by the six-fifteen to a supper of cottage-pie and stewed tinned pears.

> In the highbrow world you "get on", if you "get on" at all not so much by your literary ability as by being the life and soul of cocktail parties and kissing the bums of verminous little lions.

Of course, this can be laughed at, and one will only be annoyed if one is a socialist, nudist, feminist, commuter, or so on. But I agree with Orwell that good prose is closely connected with liberty, and with the social possibility of truth. I agree with him also (and so assemble this evidence) that

> modern writing at its worst . . . consists in gumming together long strips of words which have already been set in order by someone else, and making the results presentable by sheer humbug.

To overlook this practice in Orwell himself would be ridiculous and harmful. Now, in normal circumstances, any writer who at all frequently wrote in the manner of the examples quoted might be simply disregarded. Yet I see this paradox, this permission of such writing by a man who accepted the standards which condemn it, as part of the whole paradox of Orwell, which I wish to describe. He is genuinely baffling until one finds the key to the paradox, which I will call the paradox of the exile. For Orwell was one of a significant number of men who, deprived of a settled way of living, or of a faith, or having rejected those which were inherited, find virtue in a kind of improvised living, and in an assertion of independence. The tradition, in England, is distinguished. It attracts to itself many of the liberal virtues: empiricism, a certain integrity, frankness. It has also, as the normally contingent virtue of exile, certain qualities of perception: in particular, the ability to distinguish inadequacies in the groups which have been rejected. It gives, also, an appearance of strength, although this is largely illusory. The qualities, though salutary, are largely negative; there is an appearance of hardness (the austere criticism of hypocrisy, complacency, self-deceit), but this is usually brittle, and at times hysterical: the substance of community is lacking, and the tension, in men of high quality, is very great. Alongside the tough rejection of compromise, which gives the tradition its virtue, is the felt social impotence, the inability to form extending relationships. D. H. Lawrence, still the most intelligent of these men in our time, knew this condition and described it. Orwell may also have known it; at least he lived the rejections with a thoroughness that holds the attention.

The virtues of Orwell's writing are those we expect, and value, from this tradition as a whole. Yet we need to make a distinction between exile and vagrancy: there is usually a principle in exile, there is always only relaxation in vagrancy. Orwell, in different parts of his career, is both exile and vagrant. The vagrant, in literary terms, is the "reporter," and, where the reporter is good, his work has the merits of novelty and a certain specialized kind of immediacy. The reporter is an observer, an intermediary: it is unlikely that he will understand, in any depth, the life about which he is writing (the vagrant from his own society, or his own class, looking at another, and still inevitably from the outside). But a restless society very easily accepts this kind of achievement: at one level the report on the curious or the exotic; at another level, when the class or society is nearer the reporter's own, the perceptive critique. Most of Orwell's early work is of one of these two kinds (*Down and Out in Paris and London; The Road to Wigan Pier*). The early novels, similarly, are a kind of fictionalized report: even the best of them, *Coming Up for Air*, has more of the qualities of the virtuoso reporter (putting himself in the place of the abstract, representative figure) than of the intensity of full imaginative realization. We listen to, and go about with, Orwell's Mr Bowling; Orwell, for the most part, is evidently present, offering his report.

Now, it would be absurd to blame Orwell for this "vagrant" experience; he had good reasons for rejecting the ways of life normally open to him. But he saw that the rejection had in the end to be ratified by some principle: this was the condition of vagrancy becoming exile, which, because of his quality, he recognized as finer. The principle he chose was socialism, and *Homage to Catalonia* is still a moving book (quite apart from the political controversy it involves) because it is a record of the most deliberate attempt he ever made to become part of a believing community. Nor can such praise be modified because the attempt, in continuing terms, failed. While we are right to question the assertion of self-sufficiency, by vagrant and exile alike, we have also to recognize the complexity of what is being rejected and of what can be found. Orwell, in exploring this complexity, did work of real value.

But the principle, though affirmed, could not now (Orwell concluded) carry him directly through to actual community. It could, in fact, only be lived in controversy. Orwell's socialism became the exile's principle, which he would at any cost keep inviolate. The cost, in practice, was a partial abandonment of his own standards: he had often to curse, wildly, to keep others away, to avoid being confused with them. He did not so much attack socialism, which was safe in his mind, as socialists, who were there and might involve him. What he did attack, in socialism, was its disciplines, and, on this basis, he came to concentrate his attack on communism. His attacks on the denial of liberty are admirable: we have all, through every loyalty, to defend the basic liberties of association and expression, or we deny man. Yet, when the exile speaks of liberty, he is in a curiously ambiguous position, for while the rights in question may be called individual, the condition of their guarantee is inevitably social. The exile, because of his own personal position, cannot finally believe in any social guarantee: to him, because this is the pattern of his own living, almost all association is suspect. He fears it because he does not want to be compromised (this is often his virtue, because he is so quick to see the perfidy which certain compromises involve). Yet he fears it also because he can see no way of confirming, socially, his own individuality; this, after all, is the psychological condition of the self-exile. Thus in attacking the denial of liberty he is on sure ground; he is wholehearted in rejecting the attempts of society to involve him. When, however, in any positive way, he has to affirm liberty, he is forced to deny its inevitable social basis: all he can fall back on is the notion of an atomistic society, which will leave individuals alone. "Totalitarian" describes a certain kind of repressive social control, but, also, any real society, any adequate community, is necessarily a totality. To belong to a community is to be a part of a whole, and, necessarily, to accept, while helping to define, its disciplines. To the exile, however, society as such is totalitarian; he cannot commit himself, he is bound to stay out.

Yet Orwell was at the same time deeply moved by what he saw of avoidable or remediable suffering and poverty, and he was convinced that the means of remedy are social, involving commitment, involving association, and, to the degree that he was serious, involving himself. In his essay *Writers and Leviathan*, which he wrote for a series in *Politics and Letters*, Orwell recognized this kind of deadlock, and his solution was that in such circumstances the writer must divide: one part of himself uncommitted, the other part involved. This indeed is the bankruptcy of exile, yet it was, perhaps, inevitable. He could not believe (it is not a matter of intellectual persuasion; it is a question of one's deepest experience and response) that *any* settled way of living exists in which a man's individuality can be socially confirmed. The writer's problem, we must now realize, is only one aspect of this general problem, which has certainly, in our own time, been acute. But because we have accepted the condition of exile, for a gifted individual, as normal, we have too easily accepted the Orwell kind of analysis as masterly. It is indeed a frank and honest report, and our kind of society has tied this knot again and again; yet what is being recorded, in Orwell, is the experience of a victim: of a man who, while rejecting the consequences of an atomistic society, yet retains deeply, in himself, its characteristic mode of consciousness. At the easy levels this tension is mediated in the depiction of society as a racket; a man may even join in the racket, but he tells himself that he has no illusions about what he is doing—he keeps a secret part of himself inviolate. At the more difficult levels, with men of Orwell's seriousness, this course is impossible, and the tension cannot be discharged. The consequent strain is indeed desperate; this, more than any objective threat, is the nightmare of *1984*.

A Marxist dismisses Orwell as "petty bourgeois," but this, while one sees what it means, is too shallow. A man cannot be interpreted in terms of some original sin of class; he is where he is, and with the feelings he has; his life has to be lived with his own experience, not with someone else's. The only point about class, where Orwell is concerned, is that he wrote extensively about the English working class, and that this, because it has been influential, has to be revalued. On such matters, Orwell is the reporter again: he is often sharply observant, often again given to plausible generalization.

In thinking, from his position, of the working class primarily as a class, he assumed too readily that observation of particular working-class people was an observation of all working-class behaviour. Because, however, he looked at people at all, he is often nearer the truth than more abstract left-wing writers. His principal failure was inevitable: he observed what was evident, the external factors, and only guessed at what was not evident, the inherent patterns of feeling. This failure is most obvious in its consequences: that he did come to think, half against his will, that the working people were really helpless, that they could never finally help themselves.

In *Animal Farm*, the geniality of mood, and the existence of a long tradition of human analogies in animal terms, allow us to overlook the point that the revolution that is described is one of animals against men. The men (the old owners) were bad, but the animals, left to themselves, divide into the pigs (the hypocritical, hating politicians whom Orwell had always attacked) and the others. These others have many virtues—strength, dumb loyalty, kindliness, but there they are: the simple horse, the cynical donkey, the cackling hens, the bleating sheep, the silly cows. It is fairly evident where Orwell's political estimate lies: his sympathies are with the exploited sheep and the other stupid animals, but the issue of government lies between drunkards and pigs, and that is as far as things can go. In *1984*, the same point is clear, and the terms are now direct. The hated politicians are in charge, while the dumb mass of "proles" goes on in very much its own ways, protected by its very stupidity. The only dissent comes from a rebel intellectual: the exile against the whole system. Orwell puts the case in these terms because this is how he really saw present society, and *1984* is desperate because Orwell recognized that on such a construction the exile could not win, and then there was no hope at all. Or rather:

> If there was hope, it must lie in the proles. . . . Everywhere stood the same solid unconquerable figure, made monstrous by work and child-bearing, toiling from birth to death and still singing. Out of those mighty loins a race of conscious beings must one day come. You were the dead; theirs was the future. But you could share in that future if you kept alive the mind.

This is the conclusion of any Marxist intellectual, in specifically Marxist terms, but with this difference from at any rate some Marxists: that the proles now, like the animals, are "monstrous" and not yet "conscious"—one day they will be so, and meanwhile the exile keeps the truth alive. The only point I would make is that this way of seeing the working people is not from fact and observation, but from the pressures of feeling exiled: other people are seen as an undifferentiated mass beyond one, the "monstrous" figure. Here, again, is the paradox: that the only class in which you can put any hope is written off, in present terms, as hopeless.

I maintain, against others who have criticized Orwell, that as a man he was brave, generous, frank and good, and that the paradox which is the total effect of his work is not to be understood in solely personal terms, but in terms of the pressures of a whole situation. I would certainly insist that his conclusions have no general validity, but the fact is, in contemporary society, that good men are driven again and again into his kind of paradox, and that denunciation of them—"he . . . runs shrieking into the arms of the capitalist publishers with a couple of horror comics which bring him fame and fortune"—is arrogant and crass. We have, rather, to try to understand, in the detail of experience, how the instincts of humanity can break down under pressure into an inhuman paradox; how a great and humane tradition can seem at times, to all of us, to disintegrate into a caustic dust.

Orwell, Freud, and *1984*

Paul Roazen

George Orwell and Sigmund Freud seem mutually uncongenial figures in intellectual history. In print Orwell rarely referred to the founder of psychoanalysis. According to his friend Geoffrey Gorer, Orwell regarded psychoanalysis with mild hostility, putting it somewhat on a par with Christian Science. Another friend, Sir Richard Rees, had no recollection of Orwell's ever once mentioning Freud's name, and considered this an aspect of Orwell's "psychological incuriosity." Orwell's first wife Eileen had a little training in the academic psychology of the late 1920s and early 1930s. Even though some eminent English intellectuals were psychoanalysts in that period, Orwell evidently had no contact with them nor any interest in their subject. On the other side of the kinship that I should like to explore, Freud in all likelihood never heard of Orwell. Freud's taste did not include many of the most illustrious twentieth-century writers and artists. In his last years Freud liked to relax with a good mystery story and relished in particular Agatha Christie's *Murder on the Orient Express*. Orwell also enjoyed detective stories, and he wrote about some of their implications and source of appeal. His novels that appeared in Freud's lifetime were narrowly read and artistically not unconventional; it is Orwell's masterpiece *1984*, published in 1949, ten years after Freud's death, that retains its uncanny, horrifying—and one might say its Freudian—air.

The Freud of history was a bourgeois gentleman. The commercial imagery of his writings reflects the declassed poverty of his youth and the

From *Virginia Quarterly Review* 54, no. 4 (Autumn 1978). ©1977 by *Virginia Quarterly Review*, the University of Virginia.

middle-class character of his strivings: Freud wrote in terms of psychological "compensations," mental "balances," "investments," "expenditures," "depreciation," "speculators" and "speculations," "amortization," "transfer," "loss," and even spoke of "leasing" an analytic hour. Freud also was a bit of a snob, excessively admiring the wealth and position of someone like his disciple the Princess George, Marie Bonaparte, who was a direct descendant of Napoleon's brother Lucien. Orwell on his part made the most strenuous effort to break away from the class system of his society. He even sought to find out what it was like at the utmost bottom of the social pyramid. Going down and out in Paris and London hardly corresponded to either Freud's ambitions or his conception of himself.

Freud conceived his role as a scientist, and he rarely lost sight of the need to systematize his ideas into a comprehensive framework. Although he might seek newspaper reviews of his books, he disdained writing for the popular press. Once in 1920, as his royalties in the United States began to mount, Freud volunteered through an American nephew, a public relations specialist, to write four articles for a New York magazine. *Cosmopolitan* then offered $1,000 for the first piece, but rejected Freud's suggested title, substituting its own topic. Freud was horrified at what he saw as the dictatorship of a crass and uncultivated society and drew back with shock at the venture. As his authorized biographer Ernest Jones commented about Freud's "stinging" letter of refusal to his relative, some of Freud's "indignation emanated from feeling a little ashamed of himself at having descended from his usual standards by proposing to earn money through writing popular articles."

Unlike Freud, Orwell had no medical practice to rely on; he was an immensely hardworking journalist who sometimes had to do hack work. Orwell came to think that it was relatively easy to live by means of journalism although his book royalties, until the end of his life, remained meager. Orwell once defined a regular book reviewer as anyone who reviews at least one hundred books a year. Orwell's vision was a sustained one, yet he was not a systematic thinker. Freud and Orwell had their respective missions in life, but Orwell's had a specifically political aim. As a socialist, he was committed to class struggle. Even in his most time-bound tracts, Orwell stands out as one of the best representatives of the humane English social tradition.

Freud was reluctant to develop the political and social implications of psychoanalysis and thought that his techniques were scientific and therefore ideologically neutral. Wherever Freud "applied" psychoanalysis to society, he emphasized that his application represented merely his personal views and that others might use psychoanalytic ideas to reach different ethical conclusions. Orwell, however, became convinced that everyone is necessarily a part of social conflict. He thought that political bias is inevitable. Even in aesthetics, Orwell insisted that there can be no such thing as neutrality.

In their practical political judgments Freud and Orwell also differed. From Orwell's point of view as an opponent of all nationalisms, Freud would at best seem politically naïve; at the outset of World War I, he joined the frenzies of enthusiasm toward the Central Powers. Like other Europeans of his day, Freud thought it well that the outbreak of warfare had swept away the artificialities of the old regime. His allegiances as a cosmopolitan soon reasserted themselves, but in his old age Freud supported a clerical and authoritarian government in Austria that put down the Socialists in a civil war. Freud not only could flatter Mussolini by inscribing a copy of *Why War?* to him but entertained as a hope the mistaken idea that one of his own disciples had direct access to the Italian dictator. Nevertheless, Freud, who rarely even voted, thought of himself as apolitical. As an enemy of Franco, Orwell would at least have been pleased that in the 1930s when Freud was asked for copies of signed manuscripts to be auctioned off in behalf of the cause of the Spanish Republic, he willingly complied.

Although Freud started out as a heretic in terms of established psychology and medical practice, he gained an almost hypnotic effect on his followers and succeeded in establishing an orthodoxy which exerts its power even today, almost forty years after his death. Freud knew the power of legend, and got his own version of the history of psychoanalysis into books long before anyone else realized that his "movement" was one which would have lasting interest. When potential renegades threatened the purity of Freud's purposes, he did not hesitate to expel deviators as "heretics." Orwell was sensitive to the ways in which would-be emancipators ended up by enslaving mankind's thought. To Orwell, unorthodoxy was a necessary part of intelligent thinking. He admired heretics as those who refused to allow their consciences to be stifled by quietly accepting received wisdom. One of Orwell's most fundamental convictions was that there were too many twentieth-century religions claiming to possess "the truth."

II

Though at first glance Orwell and Freud are quite different, in many ways they are surprisingly similar. As writers, for instance, they both fascinate by being masters of an unpretentious way of expressing themselves. Freud's visual talents fulfill Orwell's dictum that "good prose is like a window pane." (Neither of them was of Lytton Strachey's persuasion: possessing a superb command of language himself, Strachey nonetheless thought that "literature was . . . a window closed tight against the racket.") At the outset of their writing careers, both Orwell and Freud lacked sales, but by the end of their lives collected editions of their works had appeared. Orwell's triumph was a personal one, while Freud depended on the support of disciples. In Freud's case his lively style can be discerned as early as adolescence; on the other hand Orwell became a conscious artist. To round out the bare bones of a comparison, both of them are known to the world by changed names: Freud gave up Sigismund for Sigmund and, more radically, Orwell had been born Eric Blair.

In their convictions Orwell and Freud had far more in common than one might suppose. Both were superlative rationalists who felt their intelligence oppressed by the weight of human stupidity. Religious belief seemed to them a particularly noxious species of nonsense. Politically, Orwell and Freud shared a suspicion of American power. Although Orwell made much more of his concern at the dangers inherent in machines, in his daily life Freud rarely relied on the use of the telephone; for both of them letter writing was an art as well as a necessity. Although Freud was far older, born in 1856 instead of 1903, each came to feel that World War I marked a watershed after which the universe was barer and more dilapidated. Freud spent the last sixteen years of his life afflicted with sickness and the approach of painful death; 1923, the year he first got cancer, is the single most important demarcation point in his mature writings. The pessimism of *1984*, Orwell's last book, has also often been traced to his intense personal suffering. Both saw themselves as outsiders in their respective societies. Both had a sense of privacy and requested that no official biography be commissioned, though in the end each family decided that the appearance of unauthorized, and supposedly misleading, biographical studies necessitated violating that request. In his lifetime Freud became the leader of a sect, and in death both men have been the centers of cults. Their archives have been jealously guarded, if not sealed, from the public's inspection.

Orwell and Freud were committed to enlightenment and the destruction of myths. They remained puritanical believers in the power and morality of honesty. Yet both—Orwell politically and Freud scientifically—were capable of deceiving themselves. While defending the cause of enlightenment, they were unable to believe fully in the reality of progress. Both cherished European civilization as a whole, retaining a special affection for England's heritage of liberties. The world before World War I was the great age of liberal bourgeois culture; but the twentieth century undermined the empires in which Orwell and Freud had been born. The Austro-Hungarian Empire broke apart earlier than the British one, yet a mood of helplessness pervades the work of both writers. In *1984* Britain has been absorbed into the United States to help make up Oceania. Therapeutically, Freud respected and worked with "breakdowns"; Orwell became convinced that while it was impossible for anyone to win, some kinds of failure were superior to others. Both men accepted the inevitability of suffering.

Orwell's socialist commitments were not collectivist but of a liberal kind; Freud had a similar moral disposition. Both Orwell and Freud were acutely sensitive to the threat to privacy posed by the conformist pressures of society. Eccentricity and individualism can be hard to sustain. Orwell's alternative title for *1984* had been *The Last Man in Europe*. In the novel "ownlife" is a specially designated crime. Winston Smith's first seditious act is diary-keeping; he buys a blank book in a junk shop and then a penholder and a bottle of ink. Reading is also solitary and therefore becomes as subversive as writing. Orwell refused to abbreviate the difficult portion of the novel where Winston Smith reads from Emmanuel Goldstein's book; Orwell had been under pressure to make cuts there from the Book-of-the-Month Club, but he stood his ground and they adopted *1984* anyway.

As prophets, Orwell and Freud shared similar aims. Both demanded the preservation of integrity within one's soul. Their basic value was the love of liberty. Freud sought to free his patients through unearthing their childhood pasts. By reinterpreting what already exists in our mental lives and through recalling past experiences, the psychoanalyst aims to release the most vivid and genuine responsiveness. But Orwell fears in *1984* that the future holds an opposite promise. As O'Brien, Winston Smith's inquisitor, predicts: "Never again will you be capable of ordinary human feeling. Everything will be dead inside you. . . . You will be hollow. We will squeeze you empty, and then we shall fill you with ourselves."

Above all, the psychologies of Orwell's *1984* and that of Freud's system are remarkably similar. Both thinkers have been accused of misanthropy; neither defends hedonism. Both are one-sidedly morbid and characteristically negative. But their pessimistic extremism rests on the skepticism of disappointed idealism; both Orwell and Freud retain a fragmentary hope that psychology can improve mankind's lot. In a painful autobiographical essay, "Such, Such Were the Joys," written in the year he began *1984*, Orwell observed that thanks to the spread of psychological knowledge it was now "harder for parents and schoolteachers to indulge their aberrations in the name of discipline." The problem for Orwell, as for Freud, was how one could ever know what someone else, in this instance a child, might be thinking. Orwell like Freud thought that the key issue was not behavior but inner feelings.

Freud held that an understanding of unconscious motivation was the central contribution of his psychology:

> He that has eyes to see and ears to hear may convince himself that no mortal can keep a secret. If his lips are silent, he chatters with his fingertips; betrayal oozes out of him at every pore. And thus the task of making conscious the most hidden recesses of the mind is one which it is quite possible to accomplish.

In *1984* Freud's knowledge of unconscious means of expression is precisely what is to be feared; one might betray oneself through a mere expression in the eyes. "The smallest thing could give you away. A nervous tic, an unconscious look of anxiety, a habit of muttering to yourself—anything that carried with it the suggestion of abnormality, of having something to hide." Orwell called it the danger of facecrime. Winston reflected: "Your worst enemy was your own nervous system. At any moment the tension inside you was liable to translate itself into some visible symptom . . . what was frightening was that the action was quite possibly unconscious." Wishfully irrational thinking, for Orwell as for Freud, became a menace.

III

In *1984* the ubiquitous telescreen threatens to invade the mind's inner self. But despite its constant spying, Winston believes that with planning it is still possible to outwit the authorities. For "with all their cleverness they had never mastered the secret of finding out what another human being was thinking." Once imprisoned, Winston concedes, the issue would grow more acute. Even then, however, he optimistically hopes that only "facts" would be extracted:

> But if the object was not to stay alive but to stay human, what difference did it ultimately make? They could not alter your feelings; for that matter you could not alter them yourself, even if you wanted to. They could lay bare in the utmost detail everything you had done or said or thought; but the inner heart, whose workings were mysterious even to yourself, remained impregnable.

Liberalism historically has defended the distinction between a person's mind and his actions; a division between inner and outer states was also a part of the rise of the theory of religious toleration. Winston is even confident that confession under coercion need be no ultimate threat to human autonomy. "Confession is not betrayal. What you say or do doesn't matter; only feelings matter." But one purpose in Orwell's writing *1984* was to expose the weakness in traditional liberal psychology. Does the existence of subjective feelings over which we have no control, and the play of mystery, reassure or undermine the liberal ideal of self-control? Freud thought that through free associations he could succeed in finding out what another human being is thinking. He too aimed to promote self-mastery. And he saw, as did Orwell, the outdatedness of any image of old-fashioned confession: "In confession the sinner tells what he knows; in analysis the neurotic has to tell more."

Once Winston gets arrested his previous assumptions undergo almost clinical testing. Freud had thought of psychoanalysis as an educative process; his treatment procedure was designed to combat resistances based on self-deception. "Psychoanalytic treatment," he once wrote, "may in general be conceived as . . . a *re-education in overcoming internal resistances*." Under arrest, however, Winston faces a formidable ordeal which turns out to be brutal: "the task of re-educating himself."

The demands on Winston are heavier than he, or pre-Freudian psychology, could have expected. "From now onwards he must not only think right; he must feel right, dream right." It would seem that under extreme stress the ideal distinction between deeds and desires becomes meaningless. O'Brien tells Winston that "the Party is not interested in the overt act: the thought is all we care about." Freud had believed that in our unconscious minds there is no difference between wishful ideas and acts; but in *1984* this hypothesis has become a working accusatory political principle. One of the terrors of captivity turns out to be that "in the eyes of the Party there was no distinction between the thought and the deed."

Thought-crime could come about in sleep-talking or by any other involuntary expression. The Thought Police of *1984* are agents whose task is inner snooping. The telescreen is sensitive enough to pick up heartbeats. Once Winston is imprisoned, his dreams, which Freud considered the royal road to the unconscious, are also open to inspection. Unlike an analytic patient, Winston is not cooperating voluntarily. But Orwell described Winston's earlier diary-keeping as a "therapy" which has not worked. According to the logic of *1984*, Winston must now undergo a more drastic treatment.

The psychology which explains O'Brien's power over Winston is

Freudian. According to psychoanalysis, neurosis binds one to the terrors one tries to master. Freud sought to understand self-destructiveness. According to him, what a man most dreads he also longs for; and what someone fears can lead to what he fears coming true. Freud called this "the fatal truth that has laid it down that flight is precisely an instrument that delivers one over to what one is fleeing from." Winston had written his diary for O'Brien. Later Winston's panic in recurrent nightmares of rats gives O'Brien the key to understanding his breaking point, the worst thing in the world according to Winston's psyche. This ultimate horror varies from individual to individual, which accounts for O'Brien's reference to the unknown terrors of the dreaded Room 101: "Everyone knows what is in Room 101."

Freud was so preoccupied with the issue of understanding another's thoughts that in the end he came to believe in telepathy, at least in the form of thought transference; one of his more committed essays on telepathy was withheld from publication until after his death. Orwell wrote in a letter in 1949: "I can't get very interested in telepathy unless it could be developed into a reliable method." Empathy, however, was one of Orwell's goals: he once objected to orthodox Marxists on the grounds that "possessing a system which appears to explain everything, they never bother to discover what is going on inside other people's heads."

If it is possible to make too much of parallels between Orwell and Freud, Winston's torture by O'Brien is clearly modeled on psychoanalytic treatment. Winston lies flat on his back as O'Brien reads his mind. To O'Brien, Winston is "a difficult case." Their time together is described as a series of "sessions." O'Brien's stated aim is to "cure" Winston, to make him "sane." As O'Brien explains to Winston: "You are mentally deranged. You suffer from a defective memory. . . . Fortunately it is curable." Winston seems to have a "disease" which gives him "delusions." O'Brien is described as having "the air of a doctor, a teacher, even a priest, anxious to explain and persuade rather than to punish." Orwell is reported by Richard Rees to have made one direct, dismissing reference to psychoanalysis: "A psychoanalyst would have to be cleverer than his patients." A terrible feature in *1984* is precisely O'Brien's intelligence: he "knew everything." To consider Winston's torture as therapy makes it even more frightening from a libertarian point of view. Even when Winston is shown in a mirror the physical wreck O'Brien has transformed him into, O'Brien insists that it is Winston who has reduced himself to such a state.

The psychoanalyst's technique of using a couch involves the patient in both social and sensory deprivation. Probably any psychotherapeutic situation, with or without a couch, evokes magical feelings. But in Freud's system of treatment, the process of overcoming self-deceptions distinctively means the arousal within the patient of resistances against the analyst; analysis then becomes a struggle. The patient makes a contract for what can, given enough sadism in an analyst and passivity in a patient, turn into an inquisition. In *1984* one of the Party's central aims had been "how to discover, against his will, what another human being is thinking." In *1984* science has almost ceased to exist; but the scientist of that time is "a mixture of psychologist and inquisitor," who does research "studying with extraordinary minuteness the meaning of facial expressions, gestures and tones of voice, and testing the truth-producing effects of drugs, shock therapy, hypnosis and physical torture." O'Brien aims not merely to destroy the Party's enemies but to change them.

Freud was naïve politically, not just in terms of day-to-day world events but about the power elements implicit in his method of treatment. He hoped that his goal of neutrality in the analyst would be enough to protect the patient from undue influence. Orwell however was exquisitely sensitive to power seeking. In *1984* he observes: "Power is in tearing human minds to pieces and putting them together in new shapes of your own choosing." In a rare reference to Freud, Orwell in an essay links him with Machiavelli, perhaps not only as a false emancipator. In the therapeutic state there are neither taboos for the individual nor legal restrictions on public authority. As a friend of individualism, Orwell worries in *1984*: "If both the past and the external world exist only in the mind, and if the mind itself is controllable—what then?" The last words of *1984* express Orwell's warning for the future; the struggle is over and Winston has conquered himself: now he loves the mythical dictator, Big Brother.

IV

Freud was a great psychologist of memory. The strength of his approach rests on the way our minds play tricks with us about our past. The distortions and selectivity of memory are, Freud held, the stuff of neurosis. The analyst should aim to correct false recollections and, through reawakening past experiences, to repair psychological damages. At the outset of *1984*, Orwell's protagonist suffers from an unintelligible childhood. Winston makes an effort to recover childhood memories; he wonders whether London has always been the same. As he forces himself to reminisce in diary-writing, new memories arise that clarify the past. At one point Winston tries to get his girlfriend Julia to collaborate in retrospection: he encourages her memory to go backwards. Winston feels that his own memory is "not satisfactorily under control," and therefore he has "furtive" knowledge that others lack. He feels in his bones "some kind of ancestral memory that things had once been different." The tormenting capacity of memory lends *1984* its nightmarish air.

Winston's sense of smell in particular evokes the past. In the Spartan world of *1984* fresh coffee succeeds in reminding him of "the half-forgotten world of his childhood." Chocolate makes him think of something he once did which he would prefer to undo, but which remains inexorably a part of his past. It takes only a whiff of a scent of chocolate to stir up a personal memory that is both "powerful and troubling." Dreams reawaken when Winston would like to forget. He takes his dreaming seriously as "a continuation of one's intellectual life . . . in which one becomes aware of facts and ideas which still seem new and valuable after one is awake." After one such dream, Winston becomes conscious why memories of his mother had been tearing at his heart; a childhood bit of greediness for chocolate on his part had preceded the disappearance of both his mother and his sister.

Winston's concern with memory is public as well as private. In the course of *1984* he goes down and out, trying to test an old man's recollections; regretfully he finds only "a rubbish heap of details" instead of a useful historical account. The Proles, who comprise the non-Party eighty-five percent of the population of Oceania, are no help in resisting tyranny. Winston bitterly comments that "where the Lottery was concerned, even people who could barely read and write seemed capable of intricate calculations and staggering feats of memory." Winston's job as an Outer Party member is in the Records Department, where he specializes in the falsification of written material. History can be manipulated and destroyed, as evidence from the past gets incinerated in "memory holes." Not only events but people as well can be made to disappear, as they are "vaporized" into oblivion. Winston fears the danger not merely of death but of annihilation. Winston knows that anyone's existence can be "denied and then forgotten."

During his captivity, the continuity of Winston's daily memories is broken. After he and O'Brien have looked at a document incriminating to the official version of the past, Winston reminds O'Brien of what they have just seen; but O'Brien flatly repudiates the memory. After lengthy interrogation and repugnant cruelty, Winston gets physical treatment for his mind. O'Brien administers what is described as "a devastating explosion . . . as though a piece had been taken out of his brain." Afterwards Winston is still occasionally troubled by "false memories"; but if he recalls anything contrary to the Party's demands, Winston can now dismiss it as a product of self-deception.

While Freud proposed therapeutically to reconstruct personal history,

Orwell feared the artificial destruction of the past. Their shared concern for memory led both to be dubious about the reliability of autobiographies; and their reticence about authorizing biographies of themselves stemmed from a similar historical skepticism. In *1984* bringing history up to date becomes one means of abolishing the past. A frightening Party slogan goes: "Who controls the past controls the future: who controls the present controls the past." The past becomes mutable, and therefore Orwell considers the future "unimaginable." If the past can be rewritten, does it retain any of its traditional reality?

Orwell tended to romanticize the advantages of the past, although his nostalgia is touched with bitterness. In *1984* the further back one goes the more there is of love, freedom, friendship, and loyalty. As Freud had thought that each of his patients carried within him the unconscious truths about himself, Winston proposes that the best books are "those that tell you what you know already." When Winston and Julia rent a room above the antique store, they try to recapture a lost London: "the room was a world, a pocket of the past where extinct animals could walk." According to Party teachings, "anything old, or for that matter anything beautiful, was always vaguely suspect." The glass paperweight Winston acquires stands for his yearning for the world of the past; the Thought Police are quick to smash it when they arrest him.

Freud was fascinated by the distant past; he collected ancient statuary and likened memories to archeological artifacts. The task of therapy was to loosen ties to the past and, by reviving early emotional experiences, to free the individual from neurotic bondages. Unlike Orwell's fearful regret that history has lost its meaning, Freud believed in the permanency of its power: "in mental life nothing which has once been formed can perish— . . . everything is somehow preserved and . . . in suitable circumstances . . . it can once more be brought to life." Freud thought that each of us carries within him a kind of resonance board, so that when we see or experience anything all our past memories give their overtones to our experience. The past lives in the present through the influence of unconscious forces. "In the unconscious nothing can be brought to an end, nothing is past or forgotten."

Whatever the differences in their approaches to the past, for Orwell as for Freud childhood is the central, though inaccessible, period in human history. Both believe that a child's responses and misperceptions are a permanent source of adult anxiety and conflict; both see childhood as the model of later enslavement and oppression. Although human beings may be peculiarly exploitable because of the inevitability of early dependencies, Freud and Orwell each value retaining the child's spontaneity and freshness. It is particularly significant for understanding Orwell's views that in *1984* normal family life has been destroyed. Children are dreadful savages eager to witness the spectacle of public hangings and horrible enough to become spies on the lookout for unorthodox thoughts in the minds of their own parents. When one reads Orwell's account of the sadism built into his own boarding school experience, a world to him of "force and fraud and secrecy," it is hard not to see the personal basis on which he later constructed the vision of *1984*.

V

Orwell's attitudes toward women in *1984* are close to Freud's. They both, for instance, conceive of mothers in terms of ideally self-sacrificing creatures. More importantly, the character of Julia combines a familiar set of idealized conceptions of feminity, which while they exalt women also denigrate them. Julia is noble and pure; she brings delicacies of food as well as sex. Yet she is incapable of Winston's intellectual effort; Julia falls asleep while he reads her portions of Goldstein's book. Orwell comments that "she only questioned the teachings of the Party when they in some way touched upon her own life," and that "the difference between truth and falsehood did not seem important to her." Winston is wary of intimacy, and links sensuality with stupidity; he tells her: "You're only a rebel from the waist downwards." Julia does not care much about reading, and her docile work on the novel-writing machines in the Fiction Department is a mark of Orwell's contempt.

Women are the most bigoted adherents of the Party, the staunchest hunters of heresy, and the most credulous believers in slogans. But Julia had hopefully thought that "they can make you say anything—*anything*—but they can't make you believe it. They can't get inside you." Whatever her inadequacies, Winston confides his guilt about his mother to Julia. Instead of emphasizing, as Freud often did, sex's capacity to enslave, the way passions can be bondage, Orwell saw love as capable of releasing one's best self. But Freud too could be idealistic about the emotional side of physical love. And just as Freud complained that modern civilization entailed new forms of nervousness, Orwell thought emotions flowed easier and better in the past. When he first sees the spot in the countryside that Julia had chosen for their rendezvous, it reminds Winston of a beautiful landscape he has long dreamt of.

Eroticism is the Party's enemy. Children are conceived solely for collective purposes. Pleasurable sexuality is a species of rebelliousness: "Desire was thought-crime." The sexual instinct is to be eradicated, the orgasm abolished. As an animal drive, sexuality constitutes a political act. *1984* has an "Anti-Sex League" and its vows of celibacy. Freud had foreseen how "two people in love, by excluding the larger society, incite its wrath." For Freud, neurotic symptoms could be understood on the model of an already aroused energy, first suppressed and then finding devious expression. In *1984* the energy blocked by privations gets transformed into the hysteria of war fever and leadership worship. Freud and Orwell repudiate any conception of ascetism as an ideal; both think that Christian sainthood is a form of escapism from the difficult demands of love and the pain of preferring some people more than others. And both grew suspicious of humanitarianism as a form of hypocrisy.

Orwell describes the prevalent atmosphere of *1984* as "controlled insanity." The power of the Party rests on its ability to dissipate discontents by turning them outwards towards Oceania's rivals, Eastasia and Eurasia. The world Orwell feared in the future was filled with irrational terrors and lunatic misunderstandings. Orwell not only considered Hitler criminally insane but was inclined to the view that it was possible to describe a whole culture as insane. In 1946 Orwell wrote that "political behavior is largely non-rational . . . the world is suffering from some kind of mental disease which must be diagnosed before it can be cured." Curiously, as skeptical as Orwell was about psychoanalysis, when confronted with Nazis, he chose to join the school of thought that considers anti-Semitism a sickness. After observing some captured Germans in 1945, Orwell fell back on the theory of neurosis; the appropriate remedy, he argued, was not punishment or revenge but some form of psychological treatment for the prisoners of war.

The language and imagery of the psychoanalytic consulting room pervade *1984*. Winston fears that he will unwillingly betray his inner conflicts through unconscious symptoms of unorthodoxy. He is a self-deceiver subject to occasional hallucinatory experiences. Orwell describes Winston's renting a room as a "lunatic" project. Irresistible impulses seize control of Winston; returning to the junk shop for antiques is seen as a form of death wish.

Although Orwell's vision in *1984* may sound extreme, he had become increasingly preoccupied with the problem of establishing truth and sanity in a universe of lies. Orthodoxy is one technique for maintaining emotional equilibrium, but Orwell rejects the option of securing sanity through lack of understanding. At the same time, Orwell disliked the idea that normality can be established by counting the number of people who share any belief. But if madness is not identical with nonconformity, what is it? Even Freud never went very far in exploring this critical line of thought. Orwell and Freud clung to the notion that there has to be some objective, external standard by which one assesses reality, perhaps because both of them were aware of the extent to which it is possible to delude oneself. Freud had stressed the way in which fantasies can becloud rationality. In *1984*, Goldstein, Big Brother, and a host of other features to life may be fictitious, the products of psychological invention; reality may become so elusive as to be defined solely by the intent of the Party.

The two percent of the population of Oceania who make up the Inner Party are held together by their common allegiance to a doctrine; the Brotherhood, the supposed forces of opposition, is also built on an indestructible form of ideology. But idealism leads to insanity. For once there are no longer any records that exist outside of human memory, and assuming that memories are mutable, then it becomes impossible to be sure of even the most paltry matter of fact. Orwell's objections to the way in which orthodox believers hold to the existence of "the truth" stemmed partly from his own uncertainty about how, under modern conditions, reality can ever be securely established. Becoming unbalanced was only one aspect of the problem confronting Orwell; being wrong was another. In the long run, Orwell and Freud were agreed, only the truth can make us free. In *1984* Orwell sardonically proposes warfare as a reliable guide against insanity; illusions are militarily dangerous, and therefore war kept Oceania attached to some semblance of truth.

For Orwell, sanity was part of one's humanity. "It was not by making yourself heard but by staying sane that you carried on the human heritage." One gathers from Orwell's essays that he considered Freud's distinctive method as suitable mainly for understanding the exceptionally perverse or for treating those chosen spirits in search of salvation, but throughout Orwell's work he preferred to be concerned with the maintenance of the average person's ordinary human decency. In *1984* two and two can be made sometimes to add up to five, and that kind of dislocation is only a portion of what the Party can accomplish. In the face of strange events and bizarre theories, Orwell had insisted in 1936 that "it *is* possible to be a normal decent person and yet to be fully alive." Freud tended to take for granted a standard of adulthood which worthy people more or less lived up to; both Freud and Orwell disdained the weaknesses of the "riff-raff," and used "grownupness" as a high form of praise.

VI

One of the triumphs of *1984* is Orwell's conception of Newspeak, a language invented not to expand but to decrease the scope of human thought. Orwell was convinced that politics and language were intimately connected, and the debasement of human dignity could take place in either of these interrelated spheres. The aim of Newspeak was to render thought-crime logically impossible; by destroying old words and creating new ones, thoughts can be so narrowed that heresy becomes unthinkable. The jargon of modern ideologies, such as nationalism, leads people to repress facts for the sake of consistency of conviction.

Doublethink is a Newspeak word for mastering reality by means of controlling memories. In *1984* old-fashioned contradictions become increasingly unsettling as apparent paradoxes dissolve under Newspeak logic. Since there are no laws, nothing can be illegal. The central principles of *1984*—war is peace, freedom is slavery, ignorance is strength—gain an eerie meaning by the end of the novel. Orwell once labelled schizophrenic "the power of holding simultaneously two beliefs which cancel out," and considered similarly pathological the manner of thinking which ignores "facts which are obvious and unalterable, and which will have to be faced sooner or later." Doublethink is described as the means by which one can hold "two contradictory beliefs in one's mind simultaneously," and accept both of them as true. In this respect doublethink is almost a parody of the psychoanalytic ideal of normality—the capacity to endure in the face of ambiguity, frustration, delay. By contrast, *1984* suggests that through neutralizing knowledge and altering the past, it becomes possible to forget that one has forgotten anything.

Moreover, doublethink is a concept which might well be applied to features of Freud's system of thought, which helps explain why Orwell, despite the resemblances between his own psychological beliefs and those of psychoanalysis, held himself aloof from Freudianism. If a former patient symptomatically recovers without the supervision of a psychoanalyst, then the recovery can be dismissed as a defensive "flight into health." But if a patient deteriorates in the course of treatment, the problem is supposed to lie in the patient's masochism, and the failure is put under the rubric of "negative therapeutic reaction." Some psychoanalytic patients have later ended up in psychiatric hospitals, or as suicides, but Freud could regard such outcomes as a tribute to the efficacy of psychoanalysis: the patients' neuroses had been "cured," only the success of the treatment had led the way to more primitive means of coping, psychosis. The whole concept of "resistance" in psychoanalysis can be readily abused; Freud's system had too many formulas that excused both analysts and patients from assuming full responsibility for their actions. In addition, while Freud was alive, he took pains to doctor the history of psychoanalysis to suit his own ideological purposes; and since his death, orthodox followers have continued the falsification of history. To take only one example, all the volumes of Freud's published correspondence, with one recent exception, have been tendentiously edited.

The psychology of *1984*, Orwell's greatest sustained piece of work, reflects concerns which are present in earlier writings. He once even wrote a novel, *A Clergyman's Daughter*, about a case of amnesia in a sexually repressed young woman. Freud himself readily acknowledged that "creative writers are valuable allies and their evidence is to be prized highly, for they are apt to know a whole host of things between heaven and earth of which our philosophy has not let us dream." Although Orwell could not endorse Freud's psychology, implicitly he came close to several key psychoanalytic tenets.

It need hardly be emphasized that in *1984* Orwell had composed a critique not only of Stalinism but of industrial trends in the rest of the world as well. But Orwell's famous novel was also published at one of the high points of Freud's influence, which may help account still further for its immediate success. In that early Cold War period, it was fashionable in the West for intellectuals to turn to individual psychology, and in particular to its depth dimensions, as an explanation and rationalization for their withdrawal from earlier radical social commitments. If human nature were as Orwell and Freud saw it, then little wonder that earlier hopes for change had remained unfulfilled. Whatever their respective politics, intellectually Orwell and Freud were iconoclasts; their differing commitments help explain their particular visions. The extent to which, despite all their differences, Orwell's psychology reveals similarities to Freud's, testifies to the pervasive influence of psychoanalysis on twentieth-century images of human nature. Comparing these two writers also helps show how Freud's insights fall within the history of ideas. A passage in Orwell about Jonathan Swift illuminates the power which a certain kind of genius can have:

> Swift did not possess ordinary wisdom, but he did possess a terrible intensity of vision, capable of picking out a single hidden truth and then magnifying it and distorting it. The durability of *Gulliver's Travels* goes to show that if the force of belief is behind it, a world-view which only just passes the test of sanity is sufficient to produce a great work of art.

Orwell's *1984* as well as Freud's psychoanalysis illustrate the principle that it is sometimes necessary to disproportion reality in order to heighten our perception of certain aspects of it.

Ingsoc Considered

Anthony Burgess

It is, without doubt, an oligarchy of refined intellects that is running Oceania. It cultivates a subtle solipsistic philosophy; it knows how to manipulate language and memory and, through these, the nature of perceived reality; it is totally aware of its reasons for wanting power. It has learned how to subdue personal ambition in the interests of collective rule. There is no Hitlerian or Stalinist cult of personality: Big Brother is an invention, a fictional personage and hence immortal, and those who are contained in him partake of his immortality. The oligarchy has learned how to reconcile opposites, not through dialectic, which is diachronic and admits absence of control over time, but through the synchronic technique of doublethink. Ingsoc is the first professional government, hence the last.

Its doctrines are based on a metaphysic, not a mere ethic. To make a political system emerge logically out of a concept of reality is, of course, as old as Plato. The tricky thing about the Ingsoc view of reality is that it is appropriate to a single mind rather than a collective one. Before the metaphysic can assume validity, a collective must learn the technique of thinking in the manner of a single mind.

Solipsism—which derives from Latin *solus* and *ipse* (lone self, self alone)—is a theory that posits reality as existing only in the self, or, more reasonably, states that only the self can be definitely known and verified. This means that nothing in the external world can be assumed to have independent existence. It goes further than mere idealism, which says that mind is real and matter no more than ideas, but does not necessarily reject

From *1985*. ©1978 by Anthony Burgess. Hutchinson, 1978.

the existence of many minds and, ultimately, the unifying mind of God. Solipsism teaches that minds other than that of the *solus ipse* cannot be proved to have existence. It does not, however, go so far as to permit temporal or spatial discontinuity within the individual mind, to deny logic, to admit contradiction or inconsistency. If the single mind is real, its memories cannot be illusions. The past is not malleable: it has true existence in the mind and cannot be altered by the present. Mathematical propositions have unchangeable validity, and two and two always make four. The collective solipsism of Ingsoc will have none of this. Two and two may sometimes be four, but they are just as likely to add up to three or five. This sounds like madness. But the Party teaches that madness is an attribute of the individual mind that will not merge itself into the collective one and accept its view of reality. Winston Smith holds fast to simple arithmetic as truth unassailable even by the Party, but part of his rehabilitation consists in learning how to be convinced—not merely to go through the motions of accepting—that two and two add up to whatever the Party says. Shakespeare, who foresaw most things, foresaw this:

> PETRUCHIO: I say it is the moon.
> KATHERINA: I know it is the moon.
> PETRUCHIO: Nay then you lie; it is the blessed sun.
> KATHERINA: Then God be blest, it is the blessed sun,
> But sun it is not, when you say it is not;
> And the moon changes even as your mind.
> What you will have it nam'd, even that it is,
> And so it shall be so for Katherine.

The self-willed Winston Smith has to be tamed, and O'Brien is his Petruchio.

The Party's solipsism is far saner—or certainly far more consistent—than anything the term was traditionally held to encompass. The *solus ipse* could be said to enclose space, but time lay outside it and was one of the conditions of its existence. But logically the single mind, if it is the only reality, must contain everything, and that includes time. It also includes logic. The senses are the mere instruments that serve the self, and they are subject to error. That sensory illusions exist none will deny: how can we distinguish between illusion and reality? It is unwise to rely at all on the evidence of the senses. The self only, that nonmaterial verifiable entity, can state what is and is not real. To confer on the self the one attribute it requires to be ultimately real—fixed, unchanging, immortal, like God—it is necessary only to make that self a collective one.

There is something in this notion of an undying, omnipotent, omniscient, all-controlling human entity which lifts the heart rather than depresses it. The history of man is the tale of an arduous struggle to control his environment, and failure always comes from the limitations of the individual, whose brain grows tired, whose body decays. Exalt the collective and diminish the individual, and history will be a procession of human triumphs. Which is precisely what the history of Ingsoc is.

If the collective is to function in the manner of a single mind, all its members or cells must agree as to what they observe or remember. The technique known as doublethink is a device for bringing individual observation and memory into line with whatever the Party decrees, at any given moment, to be the truth. It is the given moment that contains reality. The past does not determine the present; the present modifies the past. This is not so monstrous as it appears. The memory of the collective mind has to be contained in records, and it is in the nature of records to be alterable. Take it further: the past does not exist, and so we are at liberty to create it. When one created past conflicts with another, doublethink has to be brought into operation. It is formally defined in the book attributed to Emmanuel Goldstein, Oceania's necessary and hence unkillable public enemy, and entitled *The Theory and Practice of Oligarchical Collectivism*:

> Doublethink means the power of holding two contradictory beliefs in one's mind simultaneously, and accepting both of them. The Party intellectual knows in which direction his memories must be altered; he therefore knows that he is playing tricks with reality; but by the exercise of doublethink he also satisfies himself that reality is not violated. The process has to be conscious, or it would not be carried out with sufficient precision, but it has also to be unconscious, or it would bring with it a feeling of falsity and hence of guilt. Doublethink lies at the very heart of Ingsoc, since the essential act of the Party is to use conscious deception while retaining the firmness of purpose that goes with complete honesty. To tell deliberate lies while genuinely believing in them, to forget any fact that has become inconvenient, and then, when it becomes necessary again, to draw it back from oblivion for just so long as it is needed, to deny the existence of objective reality and all the while to take account of the reality which one denies —all this is indispensably necessary.

The existence of Goldstein's book—a creation of the Party as much as Goldstein himself—may be taken to be an act of doublethink of a very subtle kind. The Party is literally accusing itself of telling lies through the mouthpiece of an invented enemy. It is disclosing the motive of deception behind the telling of the truth. It is conflating two irreconcilable processes—the conscious and the unconscious. It is the repository of all virtue and yet admits the possibility of guilt. Doublethink is being employed to define doublethink.

Doublethink may not be laughed or shuddered off as a chilling fantasy of the author: Orwell knew he was doing little more than giving a formulation to a thought process that man has always found to be "indispensably necessary"—and not merely a thought process either: we are more accustomed than we know to reconciling opposites in our emotional, even our sensory, experiences. "*Odi et amo,*" said Catullus: I love and hate the same object and at the same time. Orwell himself once pointed out that meat is both delicious and disgusting. The sexual act is engaged in of the free will; at the same time one is driven to it by a biological urge; it is ecstatic, it is also bestial. Birth is the beginning of death. Man is a double creature, in whom flesh contradicts spirit and instinct opposes aspiration. Orwell recognized his own doubleness very sharply. He was both Eric Blair and George Orwell, a product of the fringe of the ruling class who tried to identify himself with the workers, an intellectual who distrusted intellectuals, a word-user who distrusted words. Doublethink, though rightly presented as an instrument of oppression, seems also a very reasonable technique. Our own attitude to doublethink is inevitably doublethinkful.

Hardly a single human experience is unequivocal. The philosophers of Ingsoc are as good as saying: We recognize that human life is partly a matter of juggling with opposites. We wish that new kind of human entity, the collective, to function as a unity. Unity of thought can only be achieved by forging a deliberate technique for dealing with contradictions. (Note that when you came to that word *forge* you had to perform a very rapid act of doublethink. You were, in a context that suggested cheating, ready to give it the meaning of falsifying a cheque or making counterfeit money. But then you had to give it the primary meaning of making, fashioning, with an aura of blacksmith honesty about it.) Let us control phenomena, not be controlled by them. Let there be total harmony between the past and the present. What is the past, that inert ill-understood mass of vague events, that it should exert an influence on the sunlit reality of now? It is a question of who is to be master.

Doublethink is a serious enough formulation of a mode of mental control, but it is also a grim joke. Orwell, like the rest of us, is sickened by the lies of politicians, but he knows that such lies rarely spring from genuine cynicism or contempt of the mob. A politician is wholly devoted to his party, and he has to find ways of making the worse cause seem the better.

He does not want to lie, but he has to. He can evade bare-faced falsehood by gobbledygook or euphemism, by ambiguity or redefinition. There is only one sin, and that is to be caught out. The people complain of high prices and unemployment, and they are told: "These are the growing pains of a new prosperity." Sir Harold Wilson, when prime minister of Britain, was asked to give evidence of economic progress under socialism. He said: "You cannot quantify an élan." The Pentagon is given to using expressions like "anticipatory retaliation," meaning unprovoked assault. The communists use the term democracy to mean the opposite of what democrats mean by it. Orwell ironically deplores a lack of system, of logic and consistency, in political utterances. Compared to the amateurish evasions of most ministers of state, doublethink has a certain nobility.

Ingsoc may be thought of as being too sure of its own strength to have to stoop to dishonesty. It does not like verbal obfuscation: it insists on the utmost clarity of expression, both written and spoken. To this end it has manufactured a special kind of English called Newspeak. This is characterized by grammatical regularity, syntactical simplicity, and a vocabulary shorn of unnecessary synonyms and confusing nuances. Strong verbs have disappeared, so that all preterites and past participles end in -ed, as in *swim, swimmed; fight, fighted; go, goed*. Comparison of adjectives is always on the pattern of *good, gooder, goodest*. Plurals always end in -s—*mans, oxes, childs*. This rationalization was perhaps bound to occur of its own accord sooner or later, without the assistance of the State, but Ingsoc, claiming total control of all human activities, has kindly speeded up the process. The limitation of vocabulary is a godsend or statesend: there are far too many words in the traditional language. *Bad* is unnecessary when we can have *ungood*, and intensifiers can be reduced to *plus* and, for greater emphasis, *doubleplus*. *Doubleplusungood* is a very efficient way of rendering "terribly or extremely bad," and *plusunlight* expresses what great darkness is really about.

But the chief aim of the Ingsoc philologists is not to prune the language to a becoming spareness so much as to make it capable of expressing State orthodoxy so wholeheartedly that no shadow of the heretical can intrude. *Free* still exists, along with *unfree* and *freeness* and *freewise*, but the notion can now only be a relative one, as in "free from pain." *Free* meaning "politically free" cannot make sense, since the concept no longer exists. A statement about political freedom, like the Declaration of Independence, cannot well be translated into Newspeak:

We hold these truths to be self-evident, that all men are created equal, that they are endowed by their creator with certain inalienable rights, that among these are life, liberty and the pursuit of happiness. That to secure these rights, Governments are instituted among men, deriving their powers from the consent of the governed. That whenever any form of Government becomes destructive of those ends, it is the right of the People to alter or abolish it, and to institute new Government.

Orwell says that the nearest one can come to a Newspeak translation is to "swallow the whole passage up in the single word *crimethink*. A full translation could only be an ideological translation, whereby Jefferson's words would be changed into a panegyric on absolute government." Let us, anyway, try:

> We say that truth writed is truth unwrited, that all mans are the same as each other, that their fathers and mothers maked them so that they are alive, free from all diseases and following not food but the feeling of having eated food. They are maked like this by their parents but Big Brother makes them like this. Big Brother cannot be killed but he is to be killed, and in his place there will be himself.

Nonsense, like saying that the sun will come out at night. Or, for that matter, that Big Brother is doubleplusungood when, by sheer definition, he cannot be.

In *1984* we are only in the initial phase of the control of thought through language. The State's three slogans are WAR IS PEACE; FREEDOM IS SLAVERY; IGNORANCE IS STRENGTH. Orwell has informed us that the term *freedom* can have no absolute, or political, meaning, and yet here it is, with just that meaning, blazoned on the State's coinage. Moreover, the State is using paradox in an untypically witty manner: it is the last kick of wit, we must suppose, before the endless night sets in. We are being told, very pithily, that war is the normal condition of the new age, as peace was of the old, and that it is through fighting the enemy that we best learn to love the tranquillity of our bondage. To be left to choose our own way of life is an intolerable burden; the agony of free choice is the clank of the chains of servitude to one's environment. The more we know the more we are a prey to the contradictions of thought; the less we know the better able are we to act. All this is true, and we bless the State for ridding us of the intolerable tyrannies of democracy. Men and women of the Party are now free to engage in intellectual games.

Winston Smith's work *is* an intellectual game, and a highly stimulating one. It consists in expressing doublethink through Newspeak. He has to correct errors in back numbers of the *Times*—meaning, in uningsoc terms, to perpetrate lies—and to compose his corrections, which often amount to full news items, in a language which, restricting semantic choice, promotes ingenuity. (Incidentally, we may ask why separate copies of the *Times* are allowed to exist, since the collection of them for destruction must be a great nuisance. Why shouldn't it appear as a wall newspaper?) The fascination is that of composing a long telegram. Indeed, Newspeak is recognizably based on press cablese. Orwell must have relished the exchange between Evelyn Waugh and the *Daily Mail*, when that great popular organ sent him to cover the conflict in Abyssinia: WHY UNNEWS—UNNEWS GOODNEWS —UNNEWS UNJOB—UPSTICK JOB ASSWISE. Newspeak is, God help us, fun. Doublethink is, God help us again, absorbing mental acrobatics. There may be dangers in living in 1984, but there is no need for dullness.

Consider the situation for eighty-five percent of the community—the proles. There is a war going on, but there is no conscription, and the only bombs that fall are dropped by the government, just to remind the population that there *is* a war going on. If consumer goods are short, that is an inevitable condition of war. There are pubs, with beer sold in litre glasses, there are cinemas, a state lottery, popular journalism and even pornography (produced mechanically by a department of the Ministry of Truth called Pornosec). There is no unemployment, there is enough money, there are no oppressive regulations—indeed, there are no laws at all. The entire population, prole and Party alike, is untroubled by crime and violence on the democratic model. One may walk the streets at night quite unmolested— except, presumably, by police cars on the pattern of Los Angeles. There are no worries about inflation. One of the major issues of our time, racial intolerance, is lacking. As Goldstein tells us, "Jews, Negroes, South Americans of pure Indian blood are to be found in the highest ranks of the Party." There are no stupid politicians, time-wasting political debates, ridiculous hustings. The government is efficient and stable. There are even measures devised to eliminate from life the old agonies of sex and the oppressions of family loyalty. No wonder the system is universally accepted. Winston Smith, in his ingenuous obsession with the liberty of being able to say that $2 + 2 = 4$, and his conviction that the entire army is out of step except himself, is a boil, a pustule, a flaw on the smooth body of the collective. It is a mark of charity on the State's part that he should be cured of his madness, not immediately vaporized as a damned nuisance.

During the Second World War, Orwell bravely wrote that neither Hitler nor his brand of socialism could be written off as sheer evil or morbidity. He saw the attractive elements in the Führer's personality as well as the appeal of a political system that had restored self-respect and national pride to a whole people. Only a man capable of appreciating the virtues of oligarchy could write a book like *1984*. Indeed, any intellectual disappointed with the wretched outcome of centuries of democracy must have a double-thinkful attitude to Big Brother. Given a chance, confronted by the spectacle of hundreds of millions living, joyfully, resignedly, or without overmuch complaint, in a condition of what the West calls servitude, the intellectual may well jump over the wall and find peace in some variety or other of Ingsoc. And the argument against oligarchical collectivism is perhaps not one based on a vague tradition of "liberty" but one derived from awareness of contradictions in the system itself.

In the cellars of the Ministry of Love, O'Brien tells Winston of the world the Party is building:

> A world of fear and treachery and torment, a world of trampling and being trampled upon, a world which will grow not less but *more* merciless as it refines itself. Progress in our world will be progress towards more pain. The old civilisations claimed that they were founded on love and justice. Ours is founded upon hatred. In our world there will be no emotions except fear, rage, triumph, and self-abasement. . . . Children will be taken from their mothers at birth, as one takes eggs from a hen. The sex instinct will be eradicated. Procreation will be an annual formality like the renewal of a ration card. We shall abolish the orgasm. Our neurologists are at work upon it now. . . . There will be no distinction between beauty and ugliness. There will be no curiosity, no enjoyment of the process of life. All competing pleasures will be destroyed. But always—do not forget this, Winston—always there will be the intoxication of power, constantly increasing and constantly growing subtler. Always, at every moment, there will be the thrill of victory, the sensation of trampling on an enemy who is helpless. If you want a picture of the future, imagine a boot stamping on a human face—forever.

Winston's heart freezes at the words, his tongue too: he cannot reply. But our reply might be: man is not like this, the simple pleasure of cruelty is not enough for him; the intellectual—for only intellectuals with, behind them, a long deprivation of power, can articulate a concept like that—demands a multiplicity of pleasures; you talk of the intoxication of power growing subtler, but it seems to me you refer to something growing simpler; this brutal simplification surely entails a diminution of the intellectual subtlety that alone can sustain Ingsoc. Pleasures cannot, in the nature of things, remain static; have you not heard of diminishing returns? It is a very static pleasure you are talking about. You speak of the abolition of the orgasm, but you seem to forget that pleasure in cruelty is a sexual pleasure. If you kill the distinction between the beautiful and the ugly, you will have no gauge for assessing the intensity of the pleasure of cruelty. But to all our objections O'Brien would reply: I speak of a new kind of human entity.

Exactly. So he does. It has nothing to do with humanity as we have known it for several millennia. The new human entity is a science fiction concept, a kind of Martian. A remarkable quantum leap is required to get from Ingsoc—which is grounded philosophically on a very old-fashioned view of reality and, politically, on familiar state oppression—to Powerman, or whatever the new concept is to be named. Moreover, this proposed "world of trampling and being trampled upon" has to be reconciled with the continuing processes of government. The complexities of running a State machine are hardly compatible with the vision—not necessarily a demented vision—of exquisitely indulged cruelty. The pleasure of power has much to do with the pleasure of government, in the variety of modes of imposing an individual or collective will on the governed. "A boot stamping on a human face—for ever"—that is a metaphor of power, but it is a metaphor inside a metaphor. Winston, hearing the eloquence with which the Ingsoc dream is propounded, thinks he hears the voice of madness—the more terrifying because it encloses his own apparent sanity. But madness never encloses sanity; only poetry, which has the surface appearance of madness, can do that. O'Brien is poeticizing. We, the readers, are chilled and thrilled, but we do not take the poem literally.

We all know that no politician, statesman or dictator seeks power for its own sake. Power is a position, a point, an eminence, a situation of control which, when total, confers pleasures which are the reward of the power—the pleasure of choosing to be feared or loved, to do harm or good, condemn or reprieve, tyrannize or bestow benefits. We recognize power when we see a capacity for choice unqualified by exterior factors. When authority is expressed solely through doing evil, then we doubt the existence of choice and hence the existence of power. The ultimate power, by definition, is God's, and this power would seem nonexistent if it were confined to condemning sinners to hell. A Caligula or a Nero is recognized as a temporary aberration, a disease that cannot hold power for long because it can choose nothing but the destructive. The evil dreams of a Marquis de Sade derive from an incapacity to achieve orgasm by any regular means, and we accept that he has no choice but to lay on the whips or the burning omelettes. He makes more sense than O'Brien's sadism freed from the need for orgasm. O'Brien is talking not of power but of a disease not clearly understood. Disease, of its nature, either kills or is cured. And if this disease is not disease but a new kind of health for a new kind of humanity—well, so be it. But we are the old kind of humanity and not greatly interested. Kill us by all means, but let us not pretend that we are being eliminated by a higher order of reality. We are merely being torn by a tiger or pulverized by a Martian deathray.

Reality is inside the collective skull of the Party: the exterior world can be ignored or shaped according to the Party's will. If the electrical supplies fail that nourish the machines of torture, what then? Is the juice, in some mystical way, still flowing? And what if the oil supplies give out? Can mind affirm that they are still there? There is no science, since the empirical process of thought has been outlawed. Technological skills are all harnessed to the making of armaments or the elimination of personal freedom. Neurologists are abolishing the orgasm, and we must assume that cognate specializations are devising other modes of killing pleasure or enhancing pain. No preventive medicine, no advances in the curing of diseases, no transplantation of organs, no new drugs. Airstrip One would be powerless to stem a strange epidemic. Of course, the decay and death of individual citizens matters little so long as the collective body flourishes. "The individual is only a cell," says O'Brien. "The weariness of the cell is the vigour of the organism. Do you die when you cut your finger-nails?" Still, this vaunted control of the outside world is bound to seem impaired when incurable disease asks the mind to get out, it has outlived its tenancy of the flesh. Of course, logically bodies may disappear altogether, and Big Brother will find himself in the position of the Church Triumphant, souls or Soul static in the empyrean for ever and ever, but with no flesh to thwack or nerves to get screaming.

Nature ignored or ill-treated has a way of expressing her resentment, as the margarine commercials used to remind us. Pollution, says the Party, does not exist. Nature will powerfully disagree. Earthquakes cannot be shrugged off with doublethink. Collective solipsism represents a hubris the gods of the natural order would be quick to punish with failed harvests and endemic syphilis. Orwell was writing at a time when the atom bomb was feared more than the destruction of the environment. Ingsoc, though, has its provenance in an even earlier time, the Wellsian one, when nature was inert and malleable and man could do with her whatever he wished.

Even the processes of linguistic change are an aspect of nature, taking place unconsciously and, it appears, autonomously. There is no guarantee that the State's creation of Newspeak could flourish impervious to gradual

p.52

semantic distortion, vowel mutation, the influence of the richer Oldspeak of the proles. If *doubleplusungood* or, with a *Macbeth* flavouring, *doubledoubleplusungood*, is applied to an ill-cooked egg, we shall need something stronger to describe a sick headache. *Unbigbrotherwise uningsocful doubledoubledoubleplusungood*, for instance. *Bigbrotherwise*, as an intensifier, can be as neutral as *bloody*. Big Brother, being the only deity, can be invoked when we hit a thumb with a hammer or get caught in the rain. This is bound to diminish him. Pejorative semantic change is a feature of all linguistic history. But— one forgets—one is dealing with a new kind of human being and a new kind of reality. We should not strictly be speculating about something that cannot happen here.

We must take *1984* not only as a Swiftian toy but as an extended metaphor of apprehension. As a projection of a possible future, Orwell's vision has a purely fragmentary validity. Ingsoc cannot come into being: it is the unrealizable ideal of totalitarianism which mere human systems unhandily imitate. It is the metaphorical power that persists: the book continues to be an apocalyptical codex of our worst fears. But why do we have these fears? We are so damnably pessimistic that we almost want Ingsoc to happen. We are scared of the State—always the State. Why?

Gamesmanship and Androcentrism in *Nineteen Eighty-Four*

Daphne Patai

Orwell's most important contribution to dystopian literature—fictional visions of "bad places"—is generally taken to be his analysis of power in
Nineteen Eighty-Four. The major twentieth-century dystopian novels produced before *Nineteen Eighty-Four* depict societies dominated by "reason,"
eugenics, and the production process. Eugene Zamyatin's *We* (1924) and
Aldous Huxley's *Brave New World* (1932), probably the best-known examples, are similar in their views of mechanized societies whose citizens are
deprived of freedom through physical and psychological conditioning. The
rulers of these societies justify their power by moral arguments; that is, they
consider their pursuit of power a means to a socially desirable end.

Early utopian fiction repeatedly uses a kind of ethnographic model to
explain the workings of the utopian society: Through long dialogues between a "native informant" and a representative of the familiar old society,
the reader is exposed not only to impressions of the new society but also to a
closely reasoned presentation of its inner logic. The dystopian literature that
begins to be abundantly produced toward the end of the nineteenth century
varies this formula: Now there is typically a scene in which the key authority figure explains the logic of domination to the rebellious protagonist.
The pattern these dialogues follow owes much to the legend of the Grand
Inquisitor in Dostoyevski's *The Brothers Karamazov* (1880). In a crucial scene
set in Seville during the Inquisition, Christ, having reappeared, is taken into
custody and brought before the Grand Inquisitor. Man, according to the

From *The Orwell Mystique*. © 1984 by Daphne Patai. University of Massachusetts Press, 1984.

Inquisitor, is weak and irrational and unable to deal with the burden of freedom. The church must therefore take this burden upon itself, providing its flock with happiness, security, and unity instead of freedom. In one way or another, this rationale for power also appears in Zamyatin's *We* and Huxley's *Brave New World*. But Orwell explicitly breaks with this pattern by presenting a vision of the immediate future in which no moral justification of any kind is offered for the control exercised by the Party. It is, in fact, precisely this lack of moral justification that is the essential feature of Orwell's novel. Other twentieth-century dystopias, such as Jack London's *Iron Heel* (1907) and, especially, Katharine Burdekin's *Swastika Night* (1937; published under the pseudonym "Murray Constantine"), also explore the fascination with power, but *Nineteen Eighty-Four* is unusual in its apparent rejection of the moral justification for the exercise of power while failing to provide any substitute rationale.

In this chapter I shall analyze the implications of this rejection and suggest that the Party's actions can best be understood as a game. The concept of play throws considerable light on O'Brien's behavior in *Nineteen Eighty-Four*, and a perspective borrowed from game theory clarifies Winston Smith's role. This approach helps us to recognize that both O'Brien and Winston are players operating from a common frame of reference, sharing fundamental values. Examining these values leads, in turn, to an analysis and critique of Orwell's androcentrism in *Nineteen Eighty-Four*. A comparison of *Nineteen Eighty-Four* with *Swastika Night*—an important but little-known antifascist dystopia from which Orwell may have borrowed—is instrumental in allowing us to note the particular constraints operating on Orwell's imagination. His unquestioning adherence to traditional definitions of masculinity continues to create obstacles and contradictions in his avowed commitments to social justice. Orwell's despair, in *Nineteen Eighty-Four*, is, I believe, the result of his inability to confront this problem.

O'Brien at Play

In a variation on the Grand Inquisitor scene in other dystopias, Orwell has O'Brien explain to Winston Smith that the answer Winston has been seeking—the "why" of the Party's pursuit of power—lies in power itself. The means have become ends: Power is pursued entirely for its own sake. O'Brien spells out for Winston precisely what power involves: "power is power over human beings." In a series of questions and answers like a catechism, O'Brien asks: "How does one man assert his power over another, Winston?" and Winston, after weeks of torture, knows the answer: "By making him suffer." O'Brien explains the implications of this: "Obedience is not enough. Unless he is suffering, how can you be sure that he is obeying your will and not his own?" The Party will always have available to it this intoxication of power, the thrill of victory; the image of the future that O'Brien presents to Winston is of a boot stamping on a human face— forever, an image borrowed from London's *Iron Heel*.

If we disregard, for a moment, the content of the activity O'Brien is involved in and concentrate instead on its form, we find that the rejection of instrumentality—that is, of activities pursued as means to an end—is an important feature of utopian fiction. William Morris, for example, in his novel *News from Nowhere* (1890), depicts a simple society that has voluntarily rejected many of the questionable gains of technology for the sake of creativity and pleasure in work. This ideal is close to the Marxist one of creative, nonalienated activity, and it implies freedom from the realm of necessity. Even utopias that do not envision such an achievement seem to share in the ideal, as we can see from their goal of an ever-decreasing workday that allows the cultivation of leisure. The more that human beings are freed from the realm of necessity, the closer they can approach the ideal of an intrinsically valuable existence.

In other words, play and not work characterizes the good life, but to understand this idea we need to go beyond the common view of play as an escape from or a compensation for the rigors of daily life, or of leisure time as the mere period of recovery that it becomes when labor predominates in life. One of the most fundamental features of games, as virtually all students of play agree, is gratuitousness or immanence. Games are ends in themselves. They are not means to further ends (except in certain ambiguous situations —for example, professional sports). One of the simplest and clearest ways to envision the lack of instrumentality in games is to focus on the constraints imposed by play—the rules of the game, in other words. Consider basketball: If the purpose of the game were merely to put balls through baskets, a ladder could be brought in or the basket could be lowered or made much larger. Clearly, the voluntarily accepted rules of the game impose difficulties or obstacles that are essential to its pursuit. The aim—to make baskets—is thus not sufficient to define this activity as play. This end can be pursued only within the framework of certain constraints that constitute the game; accepting this framework is what playing the game means. Similarly, if someone throws a ball into the basket to dislodge a knife that might fall and injure a player during the game, this act cannot properly be viewed as playing the game. The game is an activity that is intrinsically valuable and that is pursued for its own sake. But to say that games are gratuitous is not at all to say that they are without meaning. Much can be learned about a society through the study of its games, and the games played in *Nineteen Eighty-Four* are no exception.

Not all forms of play, of course, depend on contest or competition, as Roger Caillois shows in extending Huizinga's conception of play. In addition to contest or competition, which he calls *agon*, Caillois introduces three other categories of play: chance (*alea*), simulation (*mimicry*), and vertigo (*ilinx*). In *Nineteen Eighty-Four* all four categories of play appear, but it is above all the competitive game of power that is pursued. When power is pursued for its own sake, it becomes a game, and clearly it must be a competitive game for, far from being an absolute or independent abstraction, power always consists in a *relation*. In other words, the obstacle or difficulty that makes the game of power possible is another human consciousness. But not just any other consciousness, and especially not a weak one. A weak opponent in the game of power produces the same unsatisfactory victory as a weak opponent in a game of chess: For the game to be relished, a relative equality between the players is needed. This requirement explains a great deal about O'Brien's relationship to Winston Smith.

The game analogy provides a model that helps us understand the interactions within *Nineteen Eighty-Four*, but in no way should it detract from the utter seriousness with which we should view the world Orwell projects in this novel. We need first of all to free ourselves of the conventional opposition between the realm of play and the serious concerns of "real" life. Games can be serious—deadly serious—as the game-playing aspects of military combat and political machinations make abundantly clear and as Orwell's remarks on sports also reveal. In "The Sporting Spirit," an essay written in 1945, Orwell comments on the orgies of hatred generated by international sporting contests and discusses the competitive spirit in the sports that had grown most popular. He links this emphasis to the rise of nationalism, which he characterizes as "the lunatic modern habit of identifying oneself with large power units and seeing everything in terms of competitive prestige." When strong feelings of rivalry are aroused, Orwell says, "the notion of playing the game according to the rules always vanishes. People want to see one side on top and the other side humiliated, and they forget that victory gained through cheating or through the intervention of the crowd is meaningless. . . . Serious sport has nothing to do with fair play. It is bound up with hatred, jealousy, boastfulness, disregard of all rules and sadistic pleasure in witnessing violence: in other words it is war minus the shooting." Thus, in *Nineteen Eighty-Four* we see work broken up by the "play" of Two Minutes Hate and Hate Week, which reverse Orwell's description, for they involve intense hatred without the sport or, in other words, reduce the sport to the spectator's emotional response.

O'Brien's statements to Winston about the Party's single-minded passion for power have a number of implications that need to be explored. First, and most obvious, in its pursuit of power the Party is not wholly independent, for it depends on a supply of opponents. Power requires resistance: We do not speak of power over others when resistance is not present. Lack of resistance may show that power has become institutionalized, has been transformed into authority, but mere authority is not what O'Brien is describing here. Habitual obedience, as he points out, is not enough. There must be resistance—so that the powerful, in overcoming it, can experience the thrill of their power. Second, it stands to reason that the greater the resistance, the keener the pleasure in overcoming it. The Party, therefore, must want vigorous opponents, not merely cowering conformists, in order to enhance the experience of its own mastery. Here too one can see the outlines of a game, a contest, taking shape. This provides a partial answer to Philip Rahv's criticism that the world of *Nineteen Eighty-Four* is psychologically implausible. In Rahv's view, Orwell failed to distinguish between psychological and objective truth. Rahv doubts that O'Brien could live with the naked truth of power pursued for its own sake, let alone that the pursuit of power could motivate generations of Inner Party members. Evil, Rahv says, needs pseudoreligious justification; without this justification, O'Brien's motivation remains psychologically obscure and implausible. But once we see that O'Brien's pursuit of power is a game, it becomes not only more plausible but ironically appropriate as a utopian ideal. Orwell's earlier works, especially *The Road to Wigan Pier*, also reveal a marked ambivalence toward the utopian aim of freedom from labor, the realm of necessity, and it is not surprising that he satirized this ideal in the dystopian game playing of *Nineteen Eighty-Four*. In addition, game playing affords intimacy and absorption; and intimacy is not otherwise available in the world of *Nineteen Eighty-Four*. Thus, O'Brien's devotion to the task of breaking Winston has a psychologically plausible basis: The need for intimacy between men, a theme also developed in Arthur Koestler's *Darkness at Noon* (1941).

From O'Brien's point of view, life in Oceania may provide too few opportunities for experiencing power. The war hysteria—the banners and parades and public displays—is part of the status quo. One can imagine the particular pleasure Inner Party members derive from the exquisite timing of the Party's reality control. At the end of Hate Week, precisely when the delirious mass hatred of Eurasia is at its peak, it is announced that Oceania is in fact at war with Eastasia and that Eurasia is an ally. The timing is an essential part of the fun, since it heightens the Party's sense of unique domination. The proles' principal, perhaps sole, reason for living is the weekly lottery—and it is fitting, given their total lack of control over their fate, that the Party allots to them a game of chance, that is, a game that reaffirms the arbitrariness of life and the proles' lack of power. But the games pursued by the Inner Party must be more complex, for they must forever reaffirm the power of Big Brother.

 The eternal wars among Oceania, Eastasia, and Eurasia, with constantly shifting alliances that have no fundamental effect on the wars, are clearly depicted as games—as activities engaged in for their own sake but without hope of resolution. The three societies want only to prolong the game, not to arrive at an end point. At the same time, however, these wars, which define so much of life in 1984, serve a social purpose, as Goldstein's book explains. The wars are fought both to use up surplus production in a socially useless way—that is, without raising the standard of living—and to justify the eternal need for an elite group that must bear the burden of conducting the war. There are, then, reasons for the war, but these do not negate its gamelike character. All is process; the wars will presumably go on forever. But precisely because the wars serve an ulterior purpose—because they seem to justify the Party's rule—they are not occasions for the absolutely free exercise of power. In addition, they are far-off and in some sense abstract; hence they cannot provide the immediate boot-in-the-face thrill of power that the Party seeks.

With every aspect of life controlled, at least for the twelve and one-half percent of the population who are Outer Party members and who make up the group from which dissidents might arise (the proles, of course, do not count; they are so insignificant that they can be left more or less alone as they struggle to eke out an existence), the Party may in fact find itself frustrated in its exercise of power. The constant routine arrests of quickly terrorized or already converted people must be a starvation diet for those whose reason for living is the process of subjugation. It would seem that, while the Party has an ever-increasing need for strong new opponents—who alone permit the full enjoyment of power—the Party's total control of life makes such victims harder and harder to find.

A similar contradiction at the very heart of the Party's policies relates to the development of Newspeak. When the world of 1984 has evolved further, when Newspeak is perfected—as Syme, who works on the definitive Newspeak dictionary, explains—thoughtcrime will literally be impossible and there will be no thought at all in our sense of the word. When this comes about, will the Party feel its power? Or its powerlessness? The latter is the more likely outcome, for power requires the contrast, something pulling against it, an obstacle to be overcome. Since power over others is inseparable from domination, conflict is its necessary arena. How will O'Brien or his future counterpart feel powerful when there is no opposition at all, when no one can even conceive of opposition? The pursuit of power is thus a more delicate operation than O'Brien, and perhaps Orwell, imagines. Can one speak of power when the people are all lobotomized, as in Zamyatin's *We*? Against whom will O'Brien test his power in the future, when no Winstons can possibly exist? In 1984 the Party already seems to have difficulty in finding worthy opponents. Most of Winston's acquaintances, for example, are ideal Outer Party members. If they are arrested—as are Syme the dictionary maker, Ampleforth the poet, and even Parsons the total Party sycophant (who is overheard in his sleep denouncing Big Brother and is turned in by his seven-year-old daughter)—these arrests apparently serve merely as daily doses of terrorism to keep the Party's appetite for power whetted.

But let us look more closely at Winston's development as an opponent of the Party. There is no written law in Oceania; no reason for arrest need be given and no specific act need be engaged in before one can be arrested. A wrong expression, a wrong thought—perhaps any thought at all—can provide the occasion. Yet the Party has played hard to develop Winston as an opponent. He has been watched for at least seven years, as O'Brien tells him; his very dreams are known to the Party and may, in fact, have been in some way planted or induced by the Party. The Party has engaged in theatrical play—with disguises and props—and has provided Winston and Julia with a meeting place, the room above Mr. Charrington's shop. For all we know, the shop itself was there solely for Winston, a Party offering that caters to his taste for the past. O'Brien himself, in predicting (erroneously, it seems) that the Party will always have victims, tells Winston: "This drama that I have played out with you during seven years will be played out over and over again generation after generation, always in subtler forms."

O'Brien, it appears, has gone to a great deal of effort to turn Winston into a serious opponent. Even the clipping that Winston had accidentally received eleven years earlier, which provided him with the first concrete proof that the Party was falsifying history, may well have been planted by the Party. We do not know the origins of Winston's hatred for Big Brother, but we do know O'Brien's important role in focusing and strengthening Winston's opposition. O'Brien initiates Winston in the probably nonexistent Brotherhood, provides him with a copy of Goldstein's book (and later tells Winston that the book was actually written by Inner Party members, including O'Brien himself), and supports Winston's rebellion against the Party, falsely claiming to be a conspirator too. All this otherwise inexplicable deception, simply put, is an elaborate entrapment through which O'Brien creates for himself an opponent of a better quality than the run-of-the-mill arrests provide. By contrast, in Zamyatin's *We* and in Huxley's *Brave New World* there is no entrapment, no effort by the state to stage situations that will provide occasions for displays of power. Instead, the state considers its policies important for the well-being of all, and it genuinely promotes a quiescent, stable, and subdued populace. Without an ideology of power as an end in itself, there is no reason to cultivate opponents.

A further contrast between *We* and *Nineteen Eighty-Four* is that in Zamyatin's novel the protagonist is genuinely seduced into rebellious acts by a woman who leads an opposition group. In *Nineteen Eighty-Four*, however, it is not Julia who is responsible for such a seduction but rather O'Brien. Winston sees his sexual relationship with Julia, which she initiates, as a political act, a strike against the Party. It is thus made to serve a political purpose—or, in other terms, it is corrupted by the Party's all-pervasive control. Julia, in contrast to Winston, seeks sexual encounters purely for pleasure. Winston's true alliances are clear from the beginning of the novel: He hates, fears, and desires Julia and is unambivalently drawn to O'Brien. The smallest expression of interest on O'Brien's part makes Winston blossom into a conspirator, in full defiance of all common sense and caution. O'Brien's role in all this is clear and rather easy to understand. In the dialectic of power, as Hegel indicates, every master must have a slave. The master's hidden need to have his superiority recognized by the slave creates the peculiar emotional intimacy of their situation. The game of power cannot be played alone: O'Brien has to want Winston Smith and has to call him into being as a suitable opponent. Hence he waits; he waits while Winston's health improves, as a result of the affair with Julia; he waits until Winston has read some of Goldstein's book. It is easy to see why: The book fortifies Winston's commitment to objective reality and truth. It affirms that Winston is not insane. Above all, it gives him hope. He is at a sufficient height, now, from which to fall. And the harder the fall, the greater will be O'Brien's enjoyment of the game and the more intense his awareness of his own power.

Given this situation, it is not surprising that much of the novel depicts not the playing of the game itself (the encounter between Winston and O'Brien in the Ministry of Love occupies only about one-sixth of the novel) but the setting up of the conditions for play. The central encounter begins only when O'Brien and Winston appear as opposing players—when Winston discovers that he has been led into a trap and that O'Brien is his chief tormentor. Once O'Brien and Winston have been defined as opponents, the game is in full play. But what are we to make of the fact that Winston knew the truth all along—knew, that is, that O'Brien was not working for the downfall of Big Brother? Winston admits to this knowledge right after his arrest, and the subject is never alluded to again. We have examined O'Brien's role in the game, but how can we understand Winston's?

GAME THEORY AND *NINETEEN EIGHTY-FOUR*

At this point game theory can be helpful. But I should make clear that the idea of a game, in game theory, is quite different from—and in some respects the very opposite of—the game playing I have been discussing in relation to O'Brien. The play concept of games, as we have seen, has to do with activities that have intrinsic rather than instrumental value. But the emphasis of game theory is in some sense the reverse: Game theory aims at maximizing payoffs—that is, it is a highly abstract, mathematical way of determining the strategy most likely to result in the attainment of each participant's goals. Above all, game theory is of interest for its emphasis on rational decision making in interdependent situations, those situations in which two (or more) players find that the decisions of each depend in part on what the other does. It is difficult to use game theory in situations that have many variables and that offer less than perfect information about the players' motives and choices; in other words, game theory is difficult to apply in situations that are not highly controlled and carefully defined, that is, in most human situations of any complexity. But game theory provides an interesting vocabulary and helps us focus on some important issues. The absolute pursuit of power, as outlined by O'Brien, is a kind of zero-sum game. A simple model of a zero-sum game is chess, a game frequently mentioned in *Nineteen Eighty-Four*. It is a game of total conflict, in which whatever one player loses, the other gains. But zero-sum situations assume that gains and losses can be quantified, and measurements are hard to make in interactions of the kind pursued in *Nineteen Eighty-Four*. Still, it is easy to see that, for O'Brien, if there are no losers, there can also be no winners.

The implications of game theory for many fields are now being explored. One anthropologist, Walter Goldschmidt, has argued that game theory has a contribution to make to cross-cultural studies by providing us "with a way of looking at human behavior so as to find what the goals are. Put another way, game theory assumes the goals to be known and with this knowledge calculates the strategies. Social anthropologists examine the strategies and through these calculate the great unknown in exotic cultures: the values." Game theory, in this view, can provide us with the conceptual apparatus for understanding the values that lie behind the selection of certain forms of behavior. Even if we eschew the formal application of game theory, with its matrices and game trees, the approach can still help us to focus on the details of an interaction.

Orwell's novel explicitly tells us what O'Brien's motives and values are — and the analysis presented above has involved fleshing out those motives to see how his actions further certain specified ends. With Winston, however, we have almost an opposite problem: We know his actions in far greater detail, but we do not have the overriding rationale that makes sense of them all. We do not know why he is initially drawn to O'Brien or why he enters into a game with him in which, as he repeatedly says, he knows he is doomed from the start or why he interacts with O'Brien in the particular way that he does, to the point of loving and indeed almost worshiping him, even after he knows he has been trapped. Game theory assumes the rational pursuit of strategies, that is, that people's choices are rationally consistent with perceived preferences. Can we infer some overall goal from the choices Winston makes at various points in the narrative?

Orwell describes O'Brien as "a member of the Inner Party and holder of some post so important and remote that Winston had only a dim idea of its nature" and as "a large, burly man with a thick neck and a coarse, humorous, brutal face" who nonetheless seems curiously civilized. Fascinated by O'Brien, Winston entertains the hope that O'Brien's political orthodoxy is not perfect. The same scene depicts Winston's antagonism toward Julia and his suspicion that she may be an agent of the Thought Police. In view of the novel's later development, this scene reveals Winston's incredibly poor judgment of character. After the Two Minutes Hate, Winston catches O'Brien's eye and imagines he *knows* that O'Brien is thinking the same things he is: "An unmistakable message had passed. It was as though their two minds had opened and the thoughts were flowing from one into the other through their eyes. 'I am with you,' O'Brien seemed to be saying to him. 'I know precisely what you are feeling. I know all about your contempt, your hatred, your disgust. But don't worry, I am on your side!' And then the flash of intelligence was gone, and O'Brien's face was as inscrutable as everybody else's." Although we can interpret Winston's response as due in part to O'Brien's intentional deception, this explanation is not sufficient to account for Winston's special attraction toward O'Brien; for up to this time Winston knows nothing about him except that he has an unusually high status within the Inner Party. As the book unfolds, we encounter no one more powerful than O'Brien—except the mythical Big Brother himself (who is, incidentally, portrayed as of the same physical type).

We expect a contest to be provoked by the person who anticipates winning, and indeed it is O'Brien who first makes overtures to Winston by finding a pretext for having Winston come to his house. But this does not make Winston a purely passive instrument of O'Brien's will. What is of interest here is the precipitous response Winston makes to O'Brien's gesture: He feels as if he has been waiting for O'Brien's move all his life, and he is at once ready to throw himself entirely on O'Brien's mercy, to incriminate himself as an enemy of the Party. Of course, this feeling might be an indication of his heroic character and his desperation in combating Big Brother. But does the scene in O'Brien's apartment bear out such a reading? In this crucial scene, which James Connors discusses in an insightful analysis of Winston's character, Winston readily agrees to cheat, forge, blackmail, corrupt the minds of children, distribute addictive drugs, encourage prostitution, disseminate venereal diseases, murder, and throw sulfuric acid in the face of a child—all for the sake of weakening the Party. Thus Winston has no grounds for differentiating himself from the Party, as O'Brien reminds him when Winston later expresses a belief in his own moral superiority.

For the moment, it is still unclear *why* Winston is willing to act as O'Brien asks. But what is clear is that he cannot be seen merely as O'Brien's innocent victim. Winston has agreed to use others as means to his own ends, causing pain and death if necessary, and he therefore has no moral basis from which to protest when he discovers that O'Brien, in turn, is using him. Winston's very words and actions, after all, have led him to this path; so he is, we must conclude, an active participant in the game the two men are playing. This argument is one answer to the possible objection (to which I return later) that Winston enters the game unwillingly—a circumstance that would seem to violate a fundamental rule of play. As we see, although he is not fully informed, he does bear responsibility for his presence in the game. Without this element of personal responsibility, the novel would not be interesting; it would merely be mechanical. But Winston is O'Brien's accomplice; he is thereby implicated in his own downfall, for he did accept O'Brien's terms—the rules of the game, as it were—and these same rules prevail at their subsequent encounter in the Ministry of Love. By his own words and actions in O'Brien's apartment, then, Winston has entered the game. His illusion about O'Brien, about the Brotherhood, marks this stage —and, indeed, the very word "illusion" means "in play" (*in-lusio*).

There is an important sense in which O'Brien does not deceive Winston. He depicts the Brotherhood in almost exclusively negative terms, as hopeless and ineffectual. He leaves Winston with no doubt that any opposition is doomed to failure, perhaps for as long as a thousand years, that Winston will be caught, will confess, and will then die. Here we have the irony of truth told for the sake of a grand deception. Yet Winston accepts the Brotherhood as his salvation, and he agrees to all the conditions and rules set down by O'Brien. Indeed, it is Julia who first rejects separation from Winston for the sake of the Brotherhood—it is she alone who dares to interrupt O'Brien's litany to assert the claim of personal feeling. Winston, then, does agree to the game—but without recognizing its genuine configuration. As in the eternal wars among the three powers, the means are always the same and the rules are agreed on; all that changes is the identity of the opponent.

It is as important for us to understand the "why" of Winston's behavior as it is for him to understand the "why" of the Party's pursuit of absolute power. The second scene between Winston and O'Brien, in the Ministry of Love, helps to clarify Winston's motivation. We need to recognize, however, that O'Brien's total victory is not quite the foregone conclusion that he tells Winston it is. For one thing, if it were entirely predetermined, once again the pleasure of the victory would be diminished. O'Brien too is operating under some constraints. Resisters do, after all, die under torture; they do sacrifice themselves for others (as Winston knows from his own observations of women and their children), and they can even refuse to play. These options make us realize that although O'Brien can kill Winston at any time, having to do so before extracting full enjoyment from the situation would not give O'Brien his preferred outcome for the game. Winston hopes to escape with his life and his dignity. O'Brien wants his own power to be affirmed, but that goal gives him no special reason for killing Winston, and he does not care whether Winston lives or dies. Roger Caillois points out that "one does not play to win as a sure thing. The pleasure of the game is inseparable from the risk of losing." For O'Brien, obviously, losing is a relative thing; the key issue is how much power and domination he can gain over Winston. After Winston passes through the first two stages of his "reintegration"—learning and understanding—he is restored to health, strengthened and fattened for the psychological kill of the third stage, which is acceptance. When Winston hopes for death, O'Brien assures him it will come eventually; were it to come too soon, it would deprive O'Brien of a full victory.

If Winston cannot induce his own death and end both his suffering and the game, what option does he have? There is one, although he never considers it: He can refuse to play. His choices are limited. He is being defeated level by level: his belief in objective reality has crumbled; his sense of his own moral superiority has been destroyed; his body has been broken. He knows that the Party denies the possibility of martyrdom—hence the purely private torture and the mere obliteration, later on, of all signs of the victim's existence. But this last detail also suggests that the Party is aware of ways (such as martyrdom) by which its domination could be nullified. Winston learns, concretely, about the ways of the Party only through his game with O'Brien. He does not know what the Party's aim is until O'Brien explains it to him. Does his attitude change, then, once he realizes he is involved in a game of power? Can he now figure out a way to stop the game? If so, losing would be a form of winning. An unresisting "mouse" deprives the "cat" of the fun of the game. Does Winston pursue such a strategy?

Quite the contrary. In a crucial scene O'Brien tells Winston that they have beaten him and asks him whether there is even one degradation that he has not undergone. Remarkably, instead of keeping quiet and retaining his belief in his inner world, Winston at once offers it up to O'Brien as a challenge. " 'I have not betrayed Julia,' he said." At this point, if we assume the rationality of Winston's choices—that is, if we assume that his moves reflect an effort to achieve certain goals—the logic of Winston's behavior, from the novel's outset, comes into focus. It now appears that Winston cares more about winning O'Brien's recognition than about sustaining his own inner world. With this virtual challenge to O'Brien he sacrifices the latter to the former and also keeps the game going. However temporarily, Winston has gotten something out of O'Brien—recognition—and he is once again pathetically grateful for O'Brien's understanding. Winston himself acknowledges the shallowness of his rebellion against the Party. Now we see the role that his attraction to the powerful O'Brien has always played in Winston's choices. Winston has been a true opponent for O'Brien, persisting in the game partly because of his desire to partake of O'Brien's power by gaining the recognition that O'Brien alone can bestow on him. This desire explains Winston's emphasis on being understood—and it explains why he is more in O'Brien's thrall after the weeks and months of torture than before.

Since Winston undergoes no change of heart when he discovers (or, rather, acknowledges what he has always known) that O'Brien is not part of the Brotherhood, it has clearly not been the hope of participating in a rebellion that has motivated Winston from the beginning. His choices throughout the game reveal that what he is after is recognition and affirmation from O'Brien, the most powerful man he knows. If this were not so, Winston would have every reason to refuse to play, to distrust O'Brien and hope for nothing from him. That Winston, instead, continues to accord O'Brien respect and even love reveals that the two men are operating from within the same frame of reference, the same values. Both respect power, both see persons in terms of power roles—where they differ is in the degree and type of recognition they require from others. O'Brien, who is powerful, wants the stimulation of a worthy opponent to make the game interesting; Winston, who is powerless, wants the recognition that he has been a tough opponent in his way, that he has held on to his inner world despite all odds. Not surprisingly, Winston feels that O'Brien's mind contains his own. At the heart of their apparent struggle is an agreement about values, despite their disagreement about the nature of reality, and this agreement is the corruption at the core of Winston's rebellion.

It is clear, then, that in some sense Winston deserves his fate, for he is drawn to O'Brien and admires him precisely for the power and domination that O'Brien will, of course, ultimately use against him. The subtext of the novel has to do with Winston's embrace of the wrong values. Although Winston is not himself a brutal, dominant man, he wants the recognition of such a man. This conclusion, which is hinted at throughout the novel, becomes unavoidable when we see Winston's final bid for O'Brien's recognition.

Orwell's handling of the interaction between the two men illustrates what Fredric Jameson, in another context, has called the "ideological double standard." Jameson applies this term to adventure stories that allow the reader vicariously to experience and satisfy a taste for violence, while they ostensibly criticize such violence on political and social grounds. The term can be extended to cover situations in which a value system is in fact derived from the very values that are being criticized. In *Nineteen Eighty-Four* both these aspects of an ideological double standard appear, but, given that the torture scenes are not very convincing, it is the implicit adherence to a value system the book ostensibly criticizes that is the more pernicious. Curiously, Orwell was perfectly aware of this potential in literature, as his comments on Galsworthy's *Forsyte Saga* reveal: "Well, the thing that strikes one about Galsworthy is that though he's trying to be iconoclastic, he has been utterly unable to move his mind outside the wealthy bourgeois society he is attacking. With only slight modifications he takes all its values for granted." We can make the same criticism of the way Orwell depicts Winston's interaction with O'Brien.

When Winston defiantly declares that after all he has not betrayed Julia, he makes that betrayal indispensable to O'Brien's victory and shows himself once again to be the intelligent opponent-participant whose defeat O'Brien could especially relish. The "place where there is no darkness," in which Winston always imagined he would meet O'Brien, thus turns out to be the illuminated playing field of the torture chamber in which Winston gives up the last vestige of his inner world.

The peculiar intimacy between Winston and O'Brien is typical of competitive situations. In a study of the psychology of competition, Stuart Walker writes: "In few activities other than competition can a participant find a similar opportunity to assert his unique significance and simultaneously attain approval from the people he most respects. For his competitors become the people who mean the most to him." O'Brien and Winston, as we have seen, are locked together in their game, each requiring the presence of the other. It is important to realize, however, that all victories in the game of power are temporary. Mastery and domination over another human being cannot be permanent; rather, these must be continually reestablished. It is in the exercise of power that power comes into being. The eyes of the dead no longer express recognition of the superiority of the master; a corpse is merely a thing, unable to acknowledge defeat. Similarly, when the Party has finally succeeded in completely breaking—that is, converting—a human being, that person is of no further interest. This is why, once Winston has betrayed Julia, his torment is over and there are no further episodes with O'Brien.

At the end of *Nineteen Eighty-Four*, Winston is sitting alone at the Chestnut Tree Café. He is now in the position earlier occupied by the three purported Party traitors: people broken by the Party, shunned by others, playing eternal games of chess over eternal glasses of Victory Gin. The chess problem that Winston is absorbed in is an appropriate if obvious metaphor for his game with O'Brien, as Winston himself senses. He is still trying to reason, but his reasoning now leads him to conclusions that oppose his earlier ones. He notes that in an ideal chess game white always wins and white symbolizes the good, and he then inverts this observation and concludes that whatever wins must be the good, by virtue of its victory. Since Big Brother clearly always wins, as he has over Julia and Winston, Big Brother must be good. Here Orwell applies the game metaphor to the entire society of *Nineteen Eighty-Four*: All its members are engaged in a game, and in this game Big Brother always wins against the individual player.

In a sense, Winston has been forced to agree that whatever is, is right. If life is merely a neutral game, then one must, as in other games, admire the winner, regardless of who or what the victor is and how the victory comes about. Here is the ultimate logic of Winston's conversion: The victory he desired over the Party and Big Brother is transformed into the only possible victory available under the circumstances—that over himself. And this is what the last line of the novel tells us: "He had won the victory over himself. He loved Big Brother." In typical doublethink fashion, defeat is now called victory. This reversal is a logical result of Winston's acceptance of the Party's value system, which, as we have seen, underlay even his rebellion. He continues to operate according to Party models: Victory and winning are still what activity is about, but the enemy has been redefined. It is not O'Brien or Big Brother or the Party. It is Winston himself. If he cannot affect the outside world, then at least he can transform the way he thinks about it, thus achieving as much reality control as he can in the circumstances. In a world based on the idea of domination, Big Brother, being stronger, *is* always right, just as white always mates black in the ideal chess game. Winston has no choice but to worship this ultimate strength.

Orwell uses game imagery in one other important instance toward the end of the book. Winston's last memory in the novel, a memory he quickly decides is false or induced by a trick, is of a different kind of game, of play that was joy. He recalls an occasion when, as a child, he and his mother had played Snakes and Ladders. They played eight games and won four each. Surely Orwell did not think this detail, positioned just before Winston's final capitulation, would be overlooked. Winston's recollection is of an almost idyllic time, when games were not rigged, when opposing players might take turns in winning.

But, in focusing on this episode, Orwell invites us to consider once again the distinctive aspects of the games played in his novel. In three major ways, Winston and O'Brien's interaction departs from what we usually understand as playing a game. First, Winston, despite his complicity, is not a fully informed player of the game; he is more like the victim of a confidence game. Second, his participation in the game is not purely voluntary, as his sudden arrest underscores. And, finally, he cannot truly win, although he can influence the extent of his losses. This imperfect fit points to a significant feature of the game pursued in *Nineteen Eighty-Four*. Like everything else in that world, it is a perversion—a perversion of a game, similar to the perversion of intimacy, of sexuality, of family life, of nationalism, of language, and of all facets of cultural life in Oceania. But what this characteristic reveals is that even O'Brien's pursuits are subject to the peculiar limitations and inauthenticity of life in Oceania; his pleasure can only be partial, since he cannot have a perfect game partner under the prevailing rules, any more than he can have a genuine sexual intimacy or friendship. Thus the very aims and rationale of the Party are necessarily undermined by Party policy. The ideology of domination carries within itself the seeds of its own failure; it is a paradox. Orwell can successfully evoke the inescapable oppressiveness of life in Airstrip One, but he cannot convincingly explain Oceania's inner dynamics, which tend toward entropy. In this respect Philip Rahv's criticism of the novel (although not directed to this feature) is correct.

Nothing I have said so far about *Nineteen Eighty-Four* adequately explains the despair one senses at the end of the novel. The novel itself, after all, may be viewed as a demonstration of the incredible coercive forces that need to be brought to bear upon human beings to reduce them to their worst possible selves: the constant spectacles of hysteria; the sanctioning of the intimacy of pain, fear, and hatred and the prohibition of the intimacy of friendship and love; the continual material deprivation; the impediments placed in the way of genuine thought. Orwell depicts all this in great detail, while also showing us how the games played and the roles assumed within a game have everything to do with the overall values of a given society. In Oceania children participate in youth organizations called Spies, and in playing at spying they learn their social roles. Orwell was perfectly aware of the importance of such conditioning. And yet, when it comes to the essential problem of power and domination, he offers not even a hint of an etiology and instead appeals to unexamined notions of human nature.

Orwell seems to have believed in the cogency of his vision; had he not done so, the novel would not end on such a desperate note of capitulation. In a sense, then, it appears that Orwell did not carry his analysis far enough. All the perversions depicted in *Nineteen Eighty-Four* are due to domination and the pursuit of power, and Orwell sees these not as a social possibility that requires explanation but as a mysterious fact of nature. He thus reduces the desire for power to the status of a biological instinct or an unavoidable innate characteristic forever marking human nature. But the world of *Nineteen Eighty-Four* is not a world in which human nature is seen playing power games; it is specifically the story of two men committed to shared ideas of what it means to be a man and, as we have seen, dependent on each other's recognition. Only in a culture that habitually disparages the female and accepts the male as the model for the human species could it ever have gone unremarked that *Nineteen Eighty-Four* is above all the story of two men's interactions and that Julia, who is not a participant in the game of domination, presents an alternative mode of behavior.

WOMEN IN OCEANIA

In the previous section I show that the analysis of gamesmanship in *Nineteen Eighty-Four* reveals a weakness at the heart of Orwell's critique of power: a value system derived from the very thing Orwell is ostensibly criticizing. This weakness may be viewed as part of Orwell's strategy in depicting a totalitarian society, for it is unlikely that he intended Winston Smith to be viewed simply as a hero, a man not compromised by the society in which he lives. At the same time, as always happens in fiction, Orwell's text reveals his own implicit values. Although *Nineteen Eighty-Four* may indeed have been intended to warn of a possibility rather than to prophesy, as Orwell claimed, this does not alter its profoundly negative impact. What alternatives could possibly exist in a world in which domination and brutality cannot even begin to be analyzed, because they are taken for granted as part of an inevitable "human" drive for power?

In the world of *Nineteen Eighty-Four*, although men fear women because they may be spies, in general the assumptions of male centrality and female "otherness" survive intact. Julia's love for Winston makes him healthier, whereas O'Brien's attentions destroy him physically and mentally, but Winston's true alliance, as we have seen, is with O'Brien, who engages him in combat and recognizes him as a worthy opponent—a recognition that means more to Winston than Julia's love.

The romance between Julia and Winston is far less important in the novel, and occupies less space, than the "romance" between Winston and O'Brien. This is clear from the novel's beginning when Winston fears and hates (because he desires) Julia while admiring and being drawn to O'Brien. In addition, Orwell devotes far more space to the details of Winston's torture than to the details of his affair with Julia. This affair is quite possibly a concession on Orwell's part to popular literature, as well as a vehicle for setting Winston's halfhearted rebellion in motion; but Winston's true longing is for intimacy with O'Brien, the most powerful man he knows. While Winston is never depicted in serious conversation with Julia, the talks with O'Brien that accompany Winston's torture and conversion are at the heart of the novel.

The minor role attributed to women in the novel cannot be interpreted as part of Orwell's strategy of criticizing and laying bare the dynamics of totalitarianism. As readers with a different kind of sensibility, we may be aware that *Nineteen Eighty-Four* depicts a masculinized world, but Orwell did not see it this way and never made any sort of critique of the sex-role system. Although there exists within the novel a certain amount of specific information about the Party's control of sexuality and family life, there is also a wealth of detail that merely demonstrates Orwell's habitual disdain for women, evident in all his work. Thus any analysis of sex roles in *Nineteen Eighty-Four* has to begin by distinguishing between Party policy toward Party women (the proles are ignored), as articulated in the novel, and Orwell's own attitudes that inadvertently seep into the text.

In the general statements about the Party's attempt to control sexuality, Orwell adheres to a hydraulic model and believes that the Party, by suppressing sexual pleasure, can redirect the individual's energy and emotions into fanatical support of Big Brother and hatred of Oceania's enemies. Thus sex is prohibited except for procreation within marriage—and then it is supposed to be performed merely as "our duty to the Party," without love or joy. Although Orwell states that there are no laws in Oceania—so that anything and everything can be forbidden—he also notes that divorce is not permitted but separation is. Winston's marriage to Katharine—whom he considers to be the emptiest person he has ever known—was a constant trial to him, for though she had no sexual feelings she insisted on periodically performing her "duty to the Party," which Winston would have preferred to ignore altogether. Since they had no children, they were permitted to separate after a time.

Certain members of the Junior Anti-Sex League (to which Julia belongs) encourage the total prohibition of sexual intercourse and the production of children purely through artificial insemination. These children would then be brought up in institutions. But this view has not (yet) become policy. Orwell comments not at all on the meaning of such a policy for women; he includes this detail as merely another illustration of the fanaticism of Party women who support such antifamily measures. The problem of controlling family affections and allegiances is a crucial one in any totalitarian society, but Orwell does not address it beyond these few sketchy details and the description of the Spies; the child informers. He does not consider the types of conflicts such children might experience, nor does he dwell on the nature of family life given these constraints. Instead, he takes it for granted that everything works according to Party plan. Similarly, since the proles are in essence like Orwell's familiar working class, with personal loyalties and "normal" sexuality (which includes prostitution), Orwell sees no reason to dwell on them.

Orwell reveals Winston's reaction to sexual frustration but deprives his character of any insight into himself. Instead, Winston's responses become part of Orwell's indictment against women:

> Winston had disliked her [Julia] from the very first moment of seeing her. He knew the reason. It was because of the atmosphere of hockey-fields and cold baths and community hikes and general clean-mindedness which she managed to carry about with her. He disliked nearly all women, and especially the young and pretty ones. It was always the women, and above all the young ones, who were the most bigoted adherents of the Party,

> the swallowers of slogans, the amateur spies and nosers-out of
> unorthodoxy. But this particular girl gave him the impression of
> being more dangerous than most.

Orwell here dislodges the general comments about Party women so that
they are no longer attached to Winston's point of view but instead take on
the form of reliable "facts." In addition, there is no analysis of this female
fanaticism. Thus it is included not as an indication of what the Party has
done to women but only as a negative comment about women themselves,
presumably by "nature" susceptible to such fanaticism. And this despite the
fact that in Julia we have a woman who is clearly not a fanatic but who
pretends to go along with all Party manias in an effort to avoid arousing
suspicion. In this way she gains a margin of freedom for her real rebellion
against the Party. Julia's deviation from the stereotype of female fanaticism
does not evoke Orwell's analysis because she is in fact serving another
stereotype: that of the apolitical, private-minded, egocentric female. While
Winston can find a sexual "outlet" (with prostitutes and with Julia) and still
be political, single women in *Nineteen Eighty-Four* seem to be either apolitical
hedonists or sexually frustrated fanatics. Despite Orwell's sensitivity, elsewhere, to the fact that language can inhibit thought and the consequent need
to guard against one's own biases, his own language in the novel depicts
women in a way that wards off analysis while encouraging a misogynistic
nod of recognition of how women "are."

In addition, Orwell ignores what is likely to happen inside the home in
a society in which women are still viewed as inferiors and hatred runs high.
We can only guess that among the proles life is very similar to British
working-class life, about which Orwell had such ambivalent feelings (hence
Winston both admires and despises the proles). Do Oceanian men find a
release of tension and temporary assumption of masculine power through
wife beating and rape? We do not know. The "private" sphere, despite
Orwell's statement that such a thing no longer exists in 1984, is still a sealed-
off area. We do know that early in the novel Winston has fantasies of
torturing, raping, and murdering Julia—showing that this form of "outlet"
is still available in imagination at least. During the Two Minutes Hate, as
Winston watches the sheeplike face of Goldstein, the official Party enemy,
on the screen, he suddenly succeeds

> in transferring his hatred from the face on the screen to the dark-
> haired girl behind him. Vivid, beautiful hallucinations flashed
> through his mind. He would flog her to death with a rubber
> truncheon. He would tie her naked to a stake and shoot her full

of arrows like Saint Sebastian. He would ravish her and cut her throat at the moment of climax. Better than before, moreover, he realized *why* it was that he hated her. He hated her because she was young and pretty and sexless, because he wanted to go to bed with her and would never do so, because round her sweet supple waist, which seemed to ask you to encircle it with your arm, there was only the odious scarlet sash, aggressive symbol of chastity [Orwell's emphasis].

Doublethink apparently has not totally altered thought processes in Oceania; or perhaps Winston, as the rebellious hero, is meant to display the thought processes of more "normal" men. In any case, this supposedly totalitarian society seems to produce men whose thoughts and reactions often run along recognizable lines.

One of the clearest examples of the seepage into *Nineteen Eighty-Four* of Orwell's attitudes toward women occurs in the consistently negative depiction of their voices. As we have seen, this is a recurring feature of Orwell's characterization of women and therefore cannot be taken as part of the exposé of Ingsoc's negative effects on individuals. Among other examples, in the novel Orwell depicts a woman giving "a squeak of mingled fear and disgust." Mrs. Parsons has a "dreary, whining sort of voice," and the exercise leader on the telescreen in the morning yaps and barks in a "piercing female voice." There is also the "silly feminine voice" that Winston hears in the canteen and the screeching of the woman on the telescreen when he gets home. Interestingly, one male, the hated enemy Goldstein, is depicted in Party propaganda films as having a sheeplike, bleating voice.

The women in Orwell's narrative by and large appear as caricatures: They are Party secretaries, Party fanatics, Party wives like Katharine or the stereotypically helpless housewife Mrs. Parsons. They are also antisex freaks or prole prostitutes. There is no woman character in the novel comparable to Syme or Charrington or O'Brien. Although Goldstein's book explains that the Inner Party is not linked by blood and that no racial discrimination is practiced—"Jews, Negroes, South Americans of pure Indian blood are to be found in the highest ranks of the Party"—no female Inner Party members are mentioned. When Winston sees a man and a woman in the canteen, he assumes that the woman is the man's secretary. In describing Julia's work in Pornosec (which churns out machine-produced pornographic literature for prole consumption), work that is assigned to unmarried girls because they are thought to be less vulnerable than men to the corrupting influences of pornography, Orwell includes the detail that "all the workers in Pornosec, except the heads of the departments, were girls." Although Orwell reveals male dominance to be a continuing feature of life in Oceania, he does not treat this as worthy of analysis and does not raise the issue of its role in a totalitarian society. Women's options in a given society, what access they have to earning their own living and what kind of living that would be compared, for example, to becoming a man's economic dependent in exchange for housework and child-care services; how, in general, society structures women's life paths in comparison with men's—all this has everything to do with the shape of life in that society. But Orwell does not realize this, judging by his lack of attention to this problem in *Nineteen Eighty-Four*. Even Julia is a largely unexplored character, seen only in terms of her relationship with Winston.

In charting Julia's character, Orwell introduced an important deviation from several of the novels that are known to have influenced his composition of *Nineteen Eighty-Four*. Both Jack London's *Iron Heel* and Zamyatin's *We* have heroic female protagonists. But Julia, the only major female character in *Nineteen Eighty-Four*, though also a rebel, evokes yet another female stereotype. She is a rebel only "from the waist downwards," as Winston comments; she is motivated by love of pleasure—sexual pleasure—and is totally uninterested in the political dynamics of the society that oppresses her. Orwell invites the reader to view Julia in a largely negative way and to contrast her lack of seriousness with Winston's heroic attempt to understand his society. And, indeed, most critics have faithfully echoed this view of Julia, so that in comments on the novel she is routinely described as egocentric and unintelligent. A slight variation of this criticism is the condescension of Irving Howe, who refers to Julia's "charming indifference to all ideologies." Yet there are grounds for a more positive understanding of Julia's character: She does not take the Two Minutes Hate seriously, unlike Winston who gets genuinely caught up in it. She falls asleep while Winston reads to her from Goldstein's book and is skeptical about all official pronouncements. But these positive aspects of Julia's character emerge more despite Orwell's conception of her than because of it. Significantly, Julia, who is also opposing the Party, receives no attention from O'Brien. Her rebellion against the Party does not have an ideological or theoretical foundation; rather, it is grounded in her desire for pleasure and for the pursuit of a personal life. The three central characters in Orwell's novel form an interesting group, and the ways Orwell names them reflect their status within the novel. Julia has only a first name; she is an insignificant female, and Orwell in this respect follows his society's convention of considering a woman's last name a disposable, because changeable, element in an uncertain social identity. O'Brien, at the opposite pole, has only a last name, in typical masculine style. And Winston Smith, halfway between the powerless personal feminine and the powerful impersonal masculine, has a complete name, albeit an ironic one in that it combines the legendary with the commonplace.

Julia's aim is to have as much pleasure as she possibly can, which, given the oppressive world in which she must function, is no small feat. And she harms no one. O'Brien, in the key scene in his apartment, assumes that Winston speaks for both himself and Julia as he questions them about their willingness to commit all sorts of atrocities for the sake of destroying the Party. While Winston agrees to everything, Julia says nothing (she must find all this talk about throwing acid in the face of a child ridiculous)—until O'Brien asks if she and Winston are willing to be separated for the sake of destroying the Party. Only now does she break into the conversation, to say no. Here it is Julia who is revealing the commitment to purely private values that Winston so admires in the idealized maternal figures of the prole woman and his own mother, yet she is not held up for our admiration. In fact, Julia becomes yet another source of misogynistic comments. She hates her living arrangements in the hostel where she lives with thirty other women (Winston, for reasons unknown, has his own flat) and complains to Winston: "Always in the stink of women! How I hate women!"

Throughout the novel the contrast is drawn between Winston's attempt to understand his society and Julia's purely practical orientation: She is cunning, capable, mechanically oriented (she works on the machines in Pornosec)—and hedonistic, unanalytical, opportunistic. Winston's strenuous resistance to O'Brien's torture is depicted in great detail, but we are told in passing that Julia had capitulated at once to O'Brien's methods: "She betrayed you, Winston. Immediately—unreservedly. I have seldom seen anyone come over to us so promptly. You would hardly recognize her if you saw her. All her rebelliousness, her deceit, her folly, her dirty-mindedness —everything has been burned out of her. It was a perfect conversion, a textbook case," hence not worthy of either admiration or pity, unlike the tougher, more heroic (given the values of the novel) Winston. The Party's aim is to destroy men—and the more they resist, the greater the thrill of power for the Party. Julia obviously does not play this game.

The British writer Stevie Smith knew Orwell and used him as a model for two characters in her 1949 novel *The Holiday*. In a letter written in 1967, she recalls that Orwell once said to her, "Girls can't play," and she understood from this that he was referring not to sports "but rather [to] rules in general . . . and that girls were a shade anarchic and did not know or care about rules at all, with the understanding, I fancy, that they did not 'play the game.'" Though Julia describes herself as "good at games," she does not take them seriously. Instead, she puts up an elaborate front in order to more effectively pursue her own aims. She explains: "I always look cheerful and I never shirk anything. Always yell with the crowd, that's what I say. It's the only way to be safe." She displays an "open jeering hatred" of the Party and astonishes Winston by her coarse language, for Party members are not supposed to swear and Winston in general conforms to this. By adopting a narrative perspective on Julia that is largely negative, Orwell does not invite the reader to consider critically the nature of the game that is being played in *Nineteen Eighty-Four* or the implications of its rules.

Orwell's tacit assumption of a male center of gravity is evident throughout the novel in ways that reveal that it is not merely a logical consequence of his narrative focus — which is, of course, on Winston. This androcentrism is apparent even in Goldstein's book, in which the typical Party member under constant surveillance is clearly depicted as a male: "Nothing that he does is indifferent. His friendships, his relaxations, his behaviour towards his wife and children, the expression of his face when he is alone, . . . are all jealously scrutinized." The same model occurs again, when O'Brien describes the world based on pain and hatred that the Party is creating: "No one dares trust a wife or a child or a friend any longer. But in the future there will be no wives and no friends." And, of course, the very image of the future that O'Brien presents to Winston derives from a specifically male role — that of a soldier: "If you want a picture of the future, imagine a boot stamping on a human face — for ever."

This narrow perspective is reiterated in the account of the Party's control of sexuality. Prostitution, Orwell writes, is common among the proles:

> It was dangerous, but it was not a life-and-death matter. To be caught with a prostitute might mean five years in a forced-labour camp. . . . And it was easy enough, provided that you could avoid being caught in the act. The poorer quarters swarmed with women who were ready to sell themselves. Some could even be purchased for a bottle of gin, which the proles were not supposed to drink. Tacitly the Party was even inclined to encourage prostitution, as an outlet for instincts which could not be altogether suppressed. Mere debauchery did not matter very much, so long as it was furtive and joyless and only involved the women of a submerged and despised class.

Orwell here clearly has in mind male (hetero)sexuality only. Fanatical adherence to the Party is presumably enough of an "outlet" for Party women

—Julia notwithstanding. In addition, the continual wartime economy of 1984 seems likely to induce constant prostitution of women. How does Julia get the black-market items she brings to Winston? Is she really sleeping around only for fun, or also for profit? Since Inner Party members (who seem all to be male) clearly have material advantages, it makes sense to assume that there is a hidden system of distribution that draws on their power and access to scarce goods. In depicting an economy similar to that of London in the 1940s, Orwell reproduces key features of the system of which he seems to be unaware—for example, the ways in which economics affects the relations between the sexes.

That Orwell conceives of women primarily as objects, rather than as subjects in their own right, also emerges in details about Julia's behavior. Cosmetics, perfume, and traditional feminine attire are forbidden to Party members. Julia manages to find some makeup and perfume, however, and applies these one day in the secret room. Winston hardly recognizes her, such is the "improvement" in her appearance: She has become prettier and far more feminine. Julia exclaims: "And do you know what I'm going to do next? I'm going to get hold of a real woman's frock from somewhere and wear it instead of these bloody trousers. I'll wear silk stockings and high-heeled shoes! In this room I'm going to be a woman, not a Party comrade." Since Julia has no knowledge of the past or of how women used to look, the assumption seems to be that something in women's nature makes them want to decorate themselves in this way and that Julia is merely expressing her "femininity," which the Party, naturally, tries to suppress. To "be a woman" appears to involve preparing oneself as a sex object for a man. By denying such allures to women, the Party is trying to kill the sex instinct, or at least to distort and sully it. Orwell writes: "And as far as the women were concerned, the Party's efforts were largely successful."

Despite this emphasis in *Nineteen Eighty-Four* on the trappings of "feminine" appeal, Orwell is reticent on the subject of sexuality itself. Though we are told that Julia has had many affairs, not a word in the novel deals with the problem of contraception and abortion—surely vital necessities in a society as officially chaste as is Oceania. The only reference to the biological facts of reproduction occurs when Julia, very discreetly, cancels a meeting with Winston because "It's started early this time." This delicate reference to menstruation, and the assumption that it prevents intercourse (apparently the sole object of Julia and Winston's meetings), is reiterated when Winston reflects that this "particular disappointment must be a normal, recurring event" in marriage.

Judging by his novels over a fifteen-year period, there is very little change or development in Orwell's literary treatment of sex. Winston, like many of Orwell's other protagonists, is frightened of attractive women, and this fear interferes with his sexual performance. Julia is described less as a person than as a "youthful body," the possession of which fills Winston with "pride." Orwell's visions of the "golden country"—in *Nineteen Eighty-Four* as in *Coming Up for Air* and *Keep the Aspidistra Flying*—always involve the attempt at sexual "possession" of a woman and hence the affirmation of manhood. Orwell describes Winston and Julia's lovemaking in words familiar from his earlier novels: "He had pulled her down on to the ground, she was utterly unresisting, he could do what he liked with her."

Winston accepts and adopts the Party's vocabulary of "purity" and "virtue," revealing an interesting inconsistency in Orwell's conceptualization of Newspeak and doublethink. The Party, it turns out, uses the labels of purity and virtue in precisely the same way as our own bourgeois society does (or did): Chastity is pure, lack of sex is virtue. Yet instead of questioning this association, Orwell has Winston and Julia merely embrace "corruption." Winston shouts: "I hate purity, I hate goodness! I don't want virtue to exist anywhere. I want everyone to be corrupt to the bones." By reacting as he does, Winston fails to challenge the Party's hold on experience. This is also apparent in his desire to "break down that wall of virtue" that surrounds the "impregnable" Party women. Orwell does not seem aware that there is nothing either new or revolutionary in Winston's judgment that Julia's sexual promiscuity marks her as "corrupt." Thus, while situating Julia's rebelliousness in her sexuality, and in this respect going against the Party's program for women, Orwell nonetheless reproduces familiar stereotypes about women.

Countering the "corrupt" sexually active woman is the idealized maternal type, self-sacrificing and protective of her children. In *Nineteen Eighty-Four* several examples of this type appear, most notably in the portraits of Winston's mother and of the singing prole woman. Certainly Orwell views in what is for him a positive way both the prole woman, who is a vigorous and enduring breeder (whose body is repeatedly—and rhapsodically—described as "monstrous" from childbearing), and Winston's mother, who is a self-sacrificing maternal figure. Winston even feels, at some points in the novel, that hope for the future resides in these women and the values they embody. As a result, some critics have argued that Orwell attributes to women a crucial role in the maintenance of human dignity. But it is important to recognize that these female figures are not held up as the proper model for human behavior in general. Instead, they are part of Orwell's idealization of the working-class family, made up of strong, hardworking men and the maternal women who are their economic dependents. As such, these characterizations are part of the problem, not the solution.

Winston's more general statement that hope lies with the proles is undermined by the opposing view articulated in the novel, that there is no hope since the proles are unconscious. In various writings, as we have seen, Orwell attributed lack of consciousness to the oppressed: proles, natives, blacks, and women such as Winston's mother, with good hearts and limited intelligence. That Orwell idealizes women's roles within the traditional family does not contradict but indeed affirms his commitment to a society based on unequal and sexually polarized social roles. He is nostalgic for the idyllic world of conventional family life with its patriarchal power and maternal women, the world depicted in nineteenth-century American novels such as *Helen's Babies* and *Little Women*, two books Orwell especially admired. He lives in a mental space peopled largely by men, with women providing the domestic background for the activities of men, breeding and rearing the next generation, and of course valorizing the masculine role by embodying a contrasting and inferiorized "femininity." This much emerges even in the brief memories that Winston has of his mother in *Nineteen Eighty-Four*, which include a clear image of his own boyhood dominance within the family. Winston recalls how his mother sacrificed her bit of food for both her children, but Winston, unable to share, insisted on taking his little sister's portion too — and did so, forcefully.

Orwell touches on this theme of male prerogatives in his other novels as well. In *Keep the Aspidistra Flying*, as we have seen, Gordon has precisely the same sort of relationship with his sister. Orwell comments on the sacrifice of girls' interests to that of their brothers but seems to consider this merely a somewhat regrettable and unavoidable lack of fair play. He does not focus on the role such preferential treatment plays in boys' development. Similarly, in *Nineteen Eighty-Four*, Winston too has had this sort of training, and his mother's self-sacrifice and helpless protective gesture toward her starving little girl, which he apotheosizes as an instance of the old personal values that only the proles are keeping alive, can be seen negatively as an important element in the construction of a dominant masculine gender identity — that very identity that encourages not imitation of such selfless behavior but rather the abuse of one's male prerogatives against females. Hence Winston's sister, too, is to be sacrificed to his interests; this is the significance of his grabbing out of her hand the smaller piece of chocolate (less than her rightful share) that his mother had given to her.

From this memory Winston concludes not that male dominance and egocentricity need to be combated but instead that this sacrificial and helpless female behavior is an important value (For whom? one might ask) to be preserved for the future. These are clearly the patterns that continue to govern in *Nineteen Eighty-Four*, not subjected to any analysis or criticism on

Orwell's part. Instead, they are duplicated, as when Julia too brings food (real food, not the ersatz stuff Winston has been eating) to one of her meetings with Winston. Women share, men monopolize, in these rituals. Or, when men do give, in Orwell's fiction, it is as an expression of power; this is what is revealed in a scene in *Keep the Aspidistra Flying* in which Gordon finally gets some money and forces his friends to have an expensive meal that they do not want. Women's giving is taken as either tenderness, love, or mere deference to men. Men's is an assertion of dominance. In this way simple acts reproduce their socially constructed ritual significance, and gender-related inequalities are reinforced rather than challenged.

It is ironically appropriate that in *Nineteen Eighty-Four* the offering of food and femininity—tributes to the past—are made by Julia in the old-fashioned room above Mr. Charrington's shop. For the room too is a fraud, not a haven but a trap for Julia and Winston. There is no safety in the past, no escape from the world of 1984, since it is that very past that has created the masculine gender role we see at work in Orwell's dystopia. His vision thus comes full circle: no hope for the future, no escape into the past. Although in his earlier writings he occasionally argued against mistaking power hunger for a biological fact, in this novel Orwell dissociates this power hunger from the social context that alone can hope to explain it. While his novel makes it clear that life for women in Oceania is in many respects similar to their life in Orwell's own society, this is not part of his critique. Orwell assails Big Brother's domination but never notices that he is the perfect embodiment of hypertrophied masculinity.

Gender and Power in Dystopia

I focused above on women in *Nineteen Eighty-Four* because Orwell's portrayal of them, both advertently and inadvertently, helps us to understand the kind of society created in this novel. Men are everywhere in *Nineteen Eighty-Four*, yet as *men* they are invisible to Orwell. Although Orwell does not notice that the male behavior he objects to is *male* behavior, we have repeatedly seen him identifying negative characterizations of women as specifically *female* and generalizing to the entire sex. Sometimes, in fact, he does this so hastily that he misconstrues or misinterprets other writers' work. An example relevant to *Nineteen Eighty-Four* is a review that Orwell published in 1940 of Winifred Holtby's play *Take Back Your Freedom*. The play is a rather superficial psychological study of the development of a British dictator, but it is not as simpleminded as Orwell's admiring review of it suggests. Orwell seems to respond favorably to the play because his version of it fulfills his prejudices: The dictator is a latent homosexual whose mother has dominated him for too long, and Orwell's review, sounding the old theme of "blame mother," provides an opportunity to refer to yet another character as a "miserable pansy." Orwell gives the impression that it is because the dictator's mother is, as he puts it, "enlightened" that she has brought him up wrong, whereas the play indicates that it is because of her own thwarted ambitions (she had ceased to work when she married). In fact, the play makes a strong feminist argument, entirely overlooked by Orwell, about women's creativity and need to do professional work. In case the audience misses the point in relation to the dictator's mother, it is reiterated in the character of another woman, a journalist who attempts to assassinate the dictator because he has deprived her of her profession and hence made her life meaningless. Orwell does not mention this character or this reiterated theme of the negative consequences of women's exclusion from professional work. Instead, he offers his own typically misogynist version of the play and then praises it as "so remarkable in its insight."

A more important example of how Orwell's misogyny affects his reading of other writers occurs in the famous 1944 essay "Raffles and Miss Blandish." Orwell calls James Hadley Chase's *No Orchids for Miss Blandish* "a header into the cesspool" and then gives a curious misconstrual of the novel's conclusion, in which Miss Blandish, once her ordeal of rape and terror is over, commits suicide. Orwell comments: "By this time, however, she has developed such a taste for Slim's caresses that she feels unable to live without him, and she jumps out of the window of a sky-scraper." In 1945 Orwell added this footnote: "Another reading of the final episode is possible. It may mean merely that Miss Blandish is pregnant. But the interpretation I have given above seems more in keeping with the general brutality of the book." But the novel, although not providing clear details of her brutalization (unlike its treatment of male characters), does convey the depth of violence and terror experienced by Miss Blandish. She is described as dazed, drugged, cringing, unable to remember her name, with blank eyes, incapable of any gesture of resistance, terror-ridden, and, ultimately, unable to face her wealthy father. Earlier in the novel she tells Slim, her tormentor: "Why don't you get rid of me? Do you think I want to live? I don't, I tell you." And she is repeatedly described as backing miserably away from Slim.

Even if Orwell had missed all these signs of her terror (though some are echoed in *Nineteen Eighty-Four,* for example, Slim tells her he once saw a woman taken out of the river—"The rats had eaten away half her face"— and promises not to let Ma Grissom do that to her), how could he have overlooked this passage, near the novel's conclusion, describing Miss Blandish's realization "that this was the end of the nightmare and the beginning of another one. . . . Her body, racked and yearning for the peace of drugs, did not belong to her any more"? And to the very end she hopes Slim will shoot her. Orwell's footnote, quoted above, seems to rest on Miss Blandish's final words: "He's not dead. He's with me now, I know he is—at first I thought I was wrong, but I know I've got him with me. He wouldn't leave me alone, ever—and he never will." But these lines, in conjunction with the repeated description of Miss Blandish's terror and blank eyes, reveal that what has occurred is a loss of self. She is marked not just in her body but in her soul, precisely as Winston Smith ultimately will be. Her four months as Slim's prisoner have deprived her of her self, her inner world. If Orwell had been able to imagine Miss Blandish as a person, he might also have been able to give a less banal interpretation of the novel.

Orwell's essay is of interest for several other reasons. First of all, he considers Chase's prose "in the American language" to be "a brilliant piece of writing," when it is in fact full of trivial (and not always correct) clichés of American speech. This is perhaps explained by Brian Foster's observation: "In the mind of many a young Briton and his girl, American speech is the hall-mark of the tough guy and the he-man." More important, in his essay Orwell protests against the power worship and sadism evident in a novel such as *No Orchids for Miss Blandish* and raises a crucial issue: "The interconnection between sadism, masochism, success worship, power worship, nationalism and totalitarianism is a huge subject whose edges have barely been scratched, and even to mention it is considered somewhat indelicate." Orwell cannot begin to untangle this "subject," however, because he conceives of the political in a restricted sense, having to do primarily with rulers, state policies, and their overt interference in individual life. Not surprisingly, he also misses seeing the political dimensions of the gender roles apparent in *Nineteen Eighty-Four* for, while clearly depicting a world run by men preoccupied with power and domination, a world in which not a single woman is shown in a comparable role, he never addresses the issue of sex roles and gender stereotypes. *We* can see O'Brien and Winston involved in a competitive game in which affirmation of manhood is at stake, but Orwell cannot. As a result, Orwell's warning in *Nineteen Eighty-Four* seems curiously limited and off-center. The issue of gender roles lurks in the background of Orwell's text, seeping in without his apparent intention, waiting vainly to be brought forward and addressed.

Another writer in Orwell's time did address this issue in an early antifascist dystopia that in other respects strikingly foreshadows *Nineteen Eighty-Four*. In June 1937, twelve years before the publication of *Nineteen Eighty-*

Four, Swastika Night was published in London under the male pseudonym "Murray Constantine." Its author, Katharine Burdekin, had published eight previous novels, six under her own name and two as Murray Constantine. *Swastika Night* was reissued in July 1940 as a Left Book Club selection and became one of the very few works of fiction the club ever distributed to its members. Victor Gollancz, founder of the club and of the publishing house that bears his name, was also Orwell's first publisher, and *The Road to Wigan Pier* was itself a Left Book Club selection for March 1937. There is no direct evidence that Orwell was acquainted with Burdekin's novel; only the internal similarities between *Nineteen Eighty-Four* and *Swastika Night*—to be explained in a moment—suggest a connection.

Orwell, as we know, was an inveterate borrower, whose debt to writers such as Jonathan Swift, Rudyard Kipling, H. G. Wells, Jack London, Eugene Zamyatin, and James Burnham have been noted and studied by many critics. But some of Orwell's other borrowings have gone undetected. In writing *Nineteen Eighty-Four*, he also seems to have borrowed from Jim Phelan's *Jail Journey*. Reviewing Phelan's book in 1940, Orwell focuses on what he judged to be the "truly important" feature of the book, its "straightforward discussion of the sex life of prisons." Orwell considers the life described in the book to be "genuinely horrible," with sex deprivation as the main form of punishment. In smug distaste, Orwell writes: "It is perfectly well known to anyone with even a third-hand acquaintance with prisons that nearly all prisoners are chronic masturbators. In addition there is homosexuality, which is almost general in long-term jails. If Macartney's *Walls Have Mouths* [another prison memoir] is to be believed, some prisons are such hotbeds of vice that even the warders are infected."

While *Nineteen Eighty-Four* incorporates the notion that sex deprivation is at the heart of a totalitarian society, Orwell's main borrowing from Jim Phelan is along quite another line. The real importance of Phelan's book is his effective portrayal of a total institution, and a comparison of his account with Orwell's novel shows that the atmosphere of *Nineteen Eighty-Four* in fact owes much to *Jail Journey*'s depiction of prison life. It is this prison atmosphere (and not, as Anthony West has argued, Orwell's experiences as a schoolboy at St. Cyprian's) that Orwell projects onto the world at large in *Nineteen Eighty-Four*, but whereas Phelan, by cynically turning himself into a model prisoner, eventually wins his release, in Winston Smith's world no such escape is possible.

If Phelan, in *Jail Journey*, felt that the prison experience was designed to deprive him of his manhood, Burdekin's *Swastika Night*, which *Nineteen Eighty-Four* in so many respects resembles, makes the connection between masculinity and domination as elements in a socially constructed gender identity. Burdekin envisions Germany and England in the seventh century of the Hitlerian millennium. The world has been divided into the Nazi Empire (Europe and Africa) and the Japanese Empire (Asia and the Americas), which are, lamentably (given the militaristic mentality that rules both spheres), in a state of perpetual peace due to their inability to conquer one another and their unwillingness to further deplete the supply of men. Hitler is venerated as a god, and a "Reduction of Women" has occurred, by which they have been driven to an animal-like state of ignorance and are now kept purely for breeding purposes. Rape is not considered a crime, since women's former "right of rejection" was an affront to masculine vanity. Burdekin thus sees that rape is fundamentally an assault on female autonomy. All books, records, and even monuments from the past have been destroyed in an effort to make the Nazi reality the only one while wiping out traces of earlier civilizations. The Reduction of Women and the exaltation of men have, not surprisingly, led to homosexual attachments among the men, although for the German men procreation is a civic duty. A type of feudal society is in force, with German Knights as the local authorities. Christians, having wiped out all Jews at the beginning of the Nazi era, are now themselves the lowest of the low and are considered untouchable.

Like literary eutopias ("good places"), dystopias provide a framework for leveling criticism at the writer's own historical moment. Extrapolating from his own environment, Orwell arrives at an urban society that is as shabby as postwar London, and onto this he grafts Nazi and Stalinist elements. Burdekin, however, extrapolates from the romantic and medieval longings of Nazi ideologues such as Alfred Rosenberg and hence imagines a totalitarian society in which a spurious Germanic mythology with its cult of masculinity governs life and sheer ignorance is combined with brutality to form the main instruments of control. But the similarities between these two novels extend far beyond their authors' utilization of the dystopian framework. Both books depict a totalitarian regime in which individual thought has been all but eliminated and, toward this end, all information about the past has been destroyed—much more thoroughly in Burdekin's novel than in Orwell's. In both books the world is divided into distinct empires in stasis (perpetual peace in *Swastika Night*; perpetual war in *Nineteen Eighty-Four*). There is a similar hierarchy in each novel with Big Brother and der Führer at the top and the most despised groups (proles; women) at the bottom and considered to be animals. And in both societies the upper echelons have material privileges denied to others.

Furthermore, in each novel there is a rebellious protagonist who is approached by a man in a position of power (O'Brien, the Inner Party member; von Hess, the Knight). This powerful man becomes the mediator through whom the protagonist's tendency to rebel is channeled, and in each case he gives the protagonist a secret book and hence knowledge. In both novels, also, a photograph provides a key piece of evidence about the past. The protagonists, Winston and Alfred, each attempt to teach a lover/friend (Julia; Hermann) about the past by reading from the book but meet with resistance or indifference. A curious detail occurs in both novels: Julia and Hermann sleep while the secret book is read, a mark of their lack of interest and of intellectual development.

As in *Swastika Night*, in *Nineteen Eighty-Four* the secret opposition is called a "Brotherhood." Despite the apolitical inclinations of Hermann and Julia, they are each drawn into the protagonist's rebellion and ultimately destroyed by it. But Julia is a far more active rebel than Hermann, even if her rebellion is limited largely to sexual nonconformity. In each novel, too, there are official enemies—Goldstein in *Nineteen Eighty-Four*; the four arch-fiends, enemies of Hitler, in *Swastika Night*. Finally, in both novels a distortion of sexuality occurs: in *Nineteen Eighty-Four* by the prohibition of sex for pleasure; in *Swastika Night* by the degradation of women, which has turned them into animals and made love and sexual attraction a prerogative of men only. And in both novels sex is encouraged for the sake of procreation, but only with specified people.

Many of the features found in *Swastika Night* appear oddly transformed in *Nineteen Eighty-Four*. The book supposedly written by Goldstein, enemy of the Party, is a fraud, a Party plant, as is the nonexistent Brotherhood. The powerful "rebel," O'Brien, is also a fraud. Even the evidence of the photograph cannot be trusted, for it too may be planted by the Party. In sum, *Nineteen Eighty-Four* evokes a world in which lies predominate. Orwell's preoccupation with the theme of honesty and deceit (which many critics have ingenuously seen as proof of his own personal honesty) is translated into a depiction of a world in which there is nothing but lies. In the process, elements from Burdekin's attack on fascism reappear as part of an attack on socialism and communism. Even love turns out to be a fraud in *Nineteen Eighty-Four*, since betrayal invariably occurs in the well-named (in Newspeak) Ministry of Love, where love is replaced by hate and only Big Brother can emerge as the beloved.

In her ironically titled 1934 novel *Proud Man*, Burdekin criticizes Aldous Huxley's *Brave New World* for its assumption that human beings would be the same even under totally different conditions. She herself does not make that mistake. Her women, in *Swastika Night*, have indeed become like ignorant and fearful animals. Their misery seems to be their only recognizably human feature. Burdekin is also careful to show each of her male characters as seriously flawed by his environment. There are no simple heroes in her book, but there are men struggling toward understanding, and each is able to overcome his conditioning to some extent. Burdekin allows the reader some hope—that knowledge will somehow survive, that the secret book will be passed on, that a girl child may be raised with a smattering of pride. But Orwell offers only the bleak prospect of perpetual domination.

Swastika Night and Nineteen Eighty-Four are both primarily about the interactions of men. Burdekin addresses this issue in her exposé of the cult of masculinity; but Orwell, taking the worst male type as the model for the human species, seems to believe that the pursuit of power is an innate characteristic of human beings. Thus Orwell's despair and Burdekin's hope are linked to the degree of awareness that each has of gender roles and patriarchal power as social rather than biological facts.

The main contribution of Nineteen Eighty-Four to modern culture probably resides in the catchy names, such as Newspeak and doublethink, that Orwell invented for familiar phenomena. But Orwell cannot and does not provide a name for the key concept that explains the Party's preoccupation with domination, power, and violence: These are all part of what Burdekin calls the cult of masculinity. Because Burdekin is able to see and to name this phenomenon, her depiction of a totalitarian regime has a dimension lacking in Orwell's novel. What Orwell can only, helplessly, attribute to human nature, Burdekin traces to a gender polarization that can degenerate into the world of Swastika Night, with its hypertrophied masculinity on the one hand and its Reduction of Women on the other. Male egos and female bodies; male persons and female animals—these are the extremes of which an ideology of male supremacy is capable. As Orwell uses the Stalinist framework to launch his attack on totalitarianism, so Burdekin uses the Nazis as the focal point of her attack on the cult of masculinity. But she makes clear that the Nazi preoccupation with manhood was itself merely an extrapolation of a quite routine gender ideology. Unlike Orwell in his idealized portrayal of female maternal figures, Burdekin recognizes that it is but a small step from the male apotheosis of women as mothers to their degradation to mere breeding animals. In both cases women are reduced to a biological capacity, out of which is constructed an entire social identity.

While Nazi ideology overtly expressed this preoccupation with gender roles, recent studies have noted the centrality of male dominance and the "masculine principle" in all forms of fascism. Burdekin only needed to exaggerate the male supremacy she saw around her to envision Europe after seven centuries of Nazi domination as engulfed in the cult of masculinity. Thus, in *Swastika Night*, phallic pride has become the overt organizing principle of Hitlerian society. Through her dystopian fantasy, Burdekin thus gives dramatic form to something Virginia Woolf had written some years earlier: "Women have served all these centuries as looking-glasses possessing the magic and delicious power of reflecting the figure of man at twice its natural size. Without that power probably the earth would still be swamp and jungle. The glories of all our wars would be unknown."

We cannot yet define the precise contours of the connection between political power and the male gender role, but that there is such a connection is self-evident. The very fact that the exercise of power utilizes a vocabulary associated with male, but not female, gender roles points to this: Control, dominance, strength, aggression, force, authority—all these terms routinely employed in discussing power (both power *over* others, and power to *do*) also figure prominently in stereotypes of the male personality. Orwell was vaguely aware of some such connection, for he identified the label "Fascist" with "bully."

In *Nineteen Eighty-Four*, Orwell treats political power in a social vacuum, without reference to the fact that such power is exercised by males to the exclusion of females and that it is also exercised in the home. The idea of a female revolution is not in and of itself a panacea—Burdekin is right to warn, in *Proud Man*, that unless it challenges the key concept of "importance" it might simply mean a "reversal of privilege"—but to refuse to address the issue of gender roles is to circle fruitlessly around the problem, viewing it as an "essence" rather than as a particular social configuration. Although Orwell seems to believe he is attacking power in itself, in fact he never focuses on male power over females. Thus he fails to note that the abuses of power he describes are simply a further point along the male continuum of a sexually polarized society. But by departing from lofty abstractions about power hunger one arrives at less awesome and less mystifying perceptions: far from being an innate appetite mysteriously found primarily in males, power emerges as part of a prescribed and self-serving social role.

Despite the popular acclaim of *Nineteen Eighty-Four*, it is not, in the final analysis, an intellectually convincing vision. First of all, Orwell largely disregards eighty-five percent of the population—the proles—though this is generally forgotten when the novel is characterized as depicting a complete totalitarianism. And by ignoring the material contradictions that still abound in the world of Oceania (for example, someone must produce the luxury items used by Inner Party members; in this already lie the seeds of a class struggle), Orwell is able to conceive of this society as perfectly static, which is essential to his argument since it increases the feeling of entrapment and hopelessness that he sought to convey. In *Nineteen Eighty-Four* reality has *not* been brought into line with Party policy; hence the need for Newspeak, doublethink, crimestop, constant revisions of the newspapers, and so on. Despite its apparent disregard for the written word and history, the Party, in its endless revisions, reveals that it is in fact obsessed with these very things. Burdekin's solution is much simpler: Restrict literacy, promote ignorance, issue no books or papers at all. Thus there is nothing to revise, nothing to censor beyond the initial acts of destruction of the past (which, she says, took about fifty years). Whereas Orwell envisions that cities such as London in some unexplained fashion will have survived an atomic war, Burdekin's postwar society is still, seven hundred years later, organized into small towns, befitting a destroyed civilization. Each scenario involves different mechanisms of control. Orwell appears to be most interested in techniques of intellectual control. He overestimates the value of Newspeak as a static language of repression, for much more likely is the slow distortion of language that complements an entire ideology—a phrase here, a word there. Yet Orwell himself may have been aware that Newspeak was not to be taken too seriously, for in the end his novel relies on old-fashioned physical abuse and terror.

Burdekin, however, envisions a reality that has in fact been brought into line with official policy. No solipsism is necessary here, no doublethink. The habitual disparagement of women has been perfected; the possible positive meanings of female have been eliminated by the well-named Reduction of Women. Once women are reduced to an animal-like existence (but without an animal's unconsciousness), the semantic range associated with the female, which has always differed from that of the male, is reduced as well. The gender ideology that situates the male at the positive pole and the female at the negative has finally found its fulfillment in reality.

This is a more ingenious and horrifying solution. Other dystopias attempt to deal with the potentially disruptive attraction between males and females in a variety of ways. Huxley, for example, licenses sexual promiscuity and, following (though in less Taylorized form) Zamyatin's lead, opts for sexual discharge as a necessary feature of a stable system. Orwell, by contrast, prohibits sex except for the purpose of procreation, on the assumption that sexual tension could be redirected as passionate hatred of an enemy and passionate love of an abstract leader. But Burdekin follows the logic of our own language and experience and sees that these already contain the seeds for the suppression of the feminine. Given the virgin/whore, angel/demon dichotomy, all that was required in *Swastika Night* was to eliminate the idealized positive pole and then elaborate and exaggerate the demonic negative pole. The tendency to see women as animals did not need to be invented. It was already there and merely required extension. To forbid sexual love and the private life, as Orwell does in *Nineteen Eighty-Four*, is to impose rules that can be broken. It is obviously more effective to degrade an ambivalently desired object and thus stimulate horror of it and hatred for it. In this way, Burdekin insists on the fundamental continuity between her own society and her imaginative vision of its implications.

Orwell does not address the problem of how individual men react once they are deprived of their personal control over women. Since masculine power (embodied in Big Brother) is still valorized in Oceania, there is a potentially serious problem as ordinary Party men find their personal enactment of their gender role thwarted. Winston Smith, a recognizably ordinary character, may not have the same right-to-rape as the men in Burdekin's novel, but he has the same impulses. Orwell takes for granted Winston's dislike of women and anger at their sexual inaccessibility. The connection Orwell reveals between frustrated male dominance and political rebellion invites the speculation that if Winston could rape Julia he might never become a rebel. Winston's protest, such as it is, may ultimately be against the Party's usurpation of many male prerogatives. Big Brother has, in effect, deprived men of their manhood by restricting their individual domination of women. In *Nineteen Eighty-Four*, the general fear of betrayal means also that men fear women in a way that was impossible in the old days that Winston longs for. What this implies in family life is indicated by the detail that it is Mr. Parsons's seven-year-old *daughter* who turns him in to the Thought Police. "Real" masculinity officially belongs only to Big Brother and his representatives, such as O'Brien, and can be acquired by other men only through emotional alliance with these representatives. Orwell's novel thus presents us with a kind of Reduction of Men, without, however, improving the status of women. In Oceania it is not only women who must live under masculine domination. Big Brother and Inner Party members such as O'Brien monopolize the masculine gender role; they reduce men like Winston to a feminine role.

In *Nineteen Eighty-Four* Orwell develops many of the features we have already encountered in *Animal Farm*; but from the mere description of how the animals' revolution was corrupted, Orwell has moved to distinct and neatly labeled phenomena: Newspeak, doublethink, the "mutability" of the past. In keeping with his general disregard of the issue of gender roles, however, Orwell also avoids noting that the Party slogan, "Who controls the past controls the future: who controls the present controls the past," has always applied as an expression of male dominance over women. Knowledge of women's past has repeatedly disappeared into "memory holes," which is why we have needed to rediscover women's history; and why in 1983 Joanna Russ needed to publish a book called *How to Suppress Women's Writing*, to teach us again things that Virginia Woolf had taught us more than fifty years earlier in *A Room of One's Own*, and still others before her — always to have their words disappear, barred by "gatekeepers" from becoming known and recognized. Orwell is blind to the fact that the political manipulation of language did not require twentieth-century totalitarianism or modern technology. Language, including his own, was already such a weapon and had been wielded for centuries by patriarchal society. Newspeak and doublethink are not necessary to make certain things unsayable, unknowable, perhaps finally unthinkable. Ideology need only pass itself off as reality and contrary perceptions can be occluded. As long as manipulation and domination were exercised by men as a group against women as a group, Orwell saw no need to protest. When, however, the relations between the governed and the governors so altered that Orwell saw the possibility of men like himself becoming the victims of censorship and domination, these became spectacularly visible to him.

Orwell never seems conscious of the strongly masculine narrative voice evident in so much of his writing (though I believe it is a major factor in his appeal to other men); similarly, he does not seem to have been aware that his indictment of human behavior in *Nineteen Eighty-Four* is in fact an indictment of male behavior. Gamesmanship is its epitome, for here we have domination pursued for its own sake and not for any practical or material objective. Orwell could not name the ideology of which his own views were a part, but his novel has much to contribute as an allegory of hypertrophied masculinity. Given his habitual disparagement of the female and his acceptance of a male model of behavior, Orwell could not analyze the dynamics of the pursuit of power. Although he called into question many social, political, and economic conventions, he accepted learned male behavior as the human norm. While depicting an essentially masculine ideology (of domination, violence, and aggression), Orwell made the common error of confusing culture with nature. We should clearly recognize that *Nineteen Eighty-Four* contains no indictment of how human beings behave but only of how men in a particular tradition have behaved. What we know of power is linked to the male domination of society. We do not, cannot thus far, know what kind of society we would have if it were not dominated by males who are personally dominating females. No novel with female protagonists could ever have been so readily accepted as describing the generally human, but the identification of the male with the human norm is among the conventions of an androcentric society that is only now being seriously challenged.

The totalitarian nightmare, from this perspective, is neither merely a particular political configuration nor an inevitable human construct but rather a possibility inherent in the cultural polarization of superior male/inferior female. *Nineteen Eighty-Four* warns us against the incursions of big government, against the loss of freedom implicit in the pursuit of power, but it does not warn men against themselves. It does not show Winston Smith coming to an understanding of O'Brien's love of power—his expression of dominance—by recognizing the cult of frustrated masculinity at work in himself. On the contrary, the novel, like Orwell's other work, fosters disdain for women, argues for their inferior consciousness in comparison with men's, and encourages the reader to enjoy the superiority of the protagonist's conscious, protesting, male position. We are meant to admire Winston's courage and take his defeat seriously; Julia's fate hardly matters.

Far from demystifying the values implicit in his novel, Orwell takes them as a given and blames "English Socialism" on the one hand and "human nature" on the other. Orwell could have stripped bare the ideology of masculine supremacy and challenged us to confront it in all its consequences. But had he done so, he would have radically undermined his own position in the world. Instead, he chose the easier way of pessimism and despair.

The Misunderstanding of Newspeak

Roy Harris

Orwell and Ruskin did not, on the face of it, have much in common. But Ruskin once said something that Orwell might well have used as his motto for an Orwellian linguistics: "the greatest thing a human soul ever does in this world is to see something and tell what it saw in a plain way." That summarizes Orwell's theorizing about language, just as it summarizes Ruskin's theorizing about art. Let us call it the *doctrine of plain representation*. It has a simple, noble, fundamentalist ring to it.

The significance of Newspeak, the most famous figment of Orwellian linguistics, cannot be understood without reference to the doctrine of plain representation. Ruskin was doubtless thinking primarily of pictorial representation, whereas Orwell was thinking of linguistic representation. They share, however, an important set of assumptions about the concept of representation itself. The Newspeak of Orwell's novel *1984* is a language which, for certain topics, makes plain representation in the verbal mode impossible. Newspeak, in short, stands the doctrine of plain representation on its head. The pictorial equivalent for Ruskin would have been a perverse mode of drawing ("Newdraw") in which, for example, all straight lines were automatically represented as curves or wiggles—anything, in fact, *other than* straight lines. Why any artistic Establishment should bother to devise such a distorted system of pictorial representation as Newdraw is, of course, puzzling. On the other hand, where language is concerned the motivation is allegedly less obscure: it is, quite bluntly, a social and political motivation— a way of fooling most of the people most of the time.

From *Times Literary Supplement* (January 6, 1984). © 1984 by *Times Literary Supplement*.

It seems somehow significant that the term *Newspeak* itself, which Orwell introduced to the English-speaking world only thirty-five years ago, should in that relatively short time have undergone all or most of the socio-linguistic processes which validate it as part of the vocabulary of Oldspeak. What does that show? Different things, according to taste. Some will argue that it shows Orwell's linguistic worries were basically groundless, and that language obeys laws which scheming politicians and propagandists are powerless to interfere with. Others will argue, to the contrary, that it shows Orwell's linguistic instincts were basically sound, and that the subtle forms of ideological control to which the vocabulary of our public discourse is subject are powerful enough to neutralize the explosive potential of new terms which directly challenge them.

What is less controversial is that in the process of assimilation into the vocabulary of Oldspeak the word *Newspeak* has undergone emasculation. A recently published dictionary of what purports to be Newspeak includes newfangled professional jargon of any and every kind. That is not what Orwell meant. Newspeak is not Newspeak in virtue of being just new speak. Orwell was not so stupid as to think that Shakespeare had already antici-pated every lexical requirement of computer-age English.

The Newspeak of *1984* is a deliberately distorted language, designed to ensure the political enslavement of its speakers. Its aim, as Orwell describes it, is that thoughts not approved by the Party "should be literally unthink-able." That final horrendous vision at the end of the novel, where we are told the details of the programme by which Newspeak will eventually re-place Oldspeak entirely—that vision of how the deliberate manipulation of language could make freedom of thought impossible—remains one of the most chillingly powerful in the whole of English literature.

The Newspeak parable is a parable which strikes home to any audience whose native language is English. For there is a sense in which the very variety and flexibility of English as a language seems to guarantee to its users their individual right to think and speak as they please. It is no accident of history that England has never had a body equivalent to the Académie Française. The notion of a language subject to the dictatorial control of experts is as repugnant to most English people as the idea of censorship. As people who can draw upon the resources of one of the richest vocabularies in the world, we can feel nothing but repulsion for the loathsome philologist from the Ministry of Truth in *1984* who says gloatingly: "It's a beautiful thing, the destruction of words."

Orwell's parable raises in a dramatic form what is a much wider issue for any community which takes this English view of linguistic freedom: the question of our social responsibilities as language users. It is to Orwell's credit that he brought this question to the attention of a whole generation who might otherwise have overlooked it, or not been able to focus it clearly for themselves. It is all the more regrettable that his parable took the particular form it did. For Newspeak is, and is likely to remain, unsurpassed as a fictional portrayal of logophobia: and logophobia has become one of the most characteristic maladies of our times.

Certainly Orwell seems to have suffered from acute fits of it. He was not merely, as Anthony Burgess describes him, "a word-user who distrusted words" (so, to some extent, are we all) but one whose distrust of words at times bordered on the pathological. As a professional writer, he realized what he owed to his own skills of verbal manipulation. As a committed socialist, on the other hand, he instinctively disliked verbal skills as skills pre-eminently inculcated, valued and practised by a class-based educational system of which he disapproved (but of which he himself was a highly articulate product). Hence his unspoken fear that to practise verbal persuasion, to engage in verbal polemic even in the cause of socialism—or any "good" cause—might be to legitimize a trust in words which could ultimately be betrayed by words themselves. Newspeak was the public fantasy which gave fictional form to Orwell's private nightmare. But this fantasy has a psychological validity and cultural significance which go far beyond the particular circumstances of Orwell's dilemma.

Logophobia is not an exclusively twentieth-century phenomenon. It goes back at least as far as the Greek philosopher Cratylus, whose logophobia was so acute that eventually, we are told, he renounced the use of words as a mode of expression altogether. Orwell was by no means so desperate a case: he could not afford to be. What makes him such a typical representative of twentieth-century logophobia (as distinct from, say, the more esoteric logophobia of the early Wittgenstein or the more hindsighted variety of Marshall McLuhan) is his ultimate faith in the aforementioned doctrine of plain representation.

Orwellian logophobia is based on two interconnected doubts about the trustworthiness of the connection between words and meaning. One is that instead of revealing what is meant, words may be used to obscure or conceal it. The other is that instead of revealing what is meant, words may be used to misrepresent it. Hence the generalized form which Orwell's nightmare takes—the postulation of a language which has been "doctored" in such a way as to deceive its users systematically about certain social and political aspects of the world in which they live, and furthermore, "doctored" in such a way as to make it impossible for the language users themselves to detect the deception.

The fears underlying this logophobic extrapolation are based on Orwell's disgust at instances of what he saw as linguistic dishonesty and deception. This revulsion comes out strongly in some of his most vigorous writing. "Defenceless villages are bombarded from the air, the inhabitants driven out into the countryside, the cattle machine-gunned, the huts set on fire with incendiary bullets; this is called *pacification*." The Vietnam generation did not need to find the words: Orwell had already said it for them.

Unfortunately, Orwell's abhorrence of the way man's inhumanity to man can be concealed behind all kinds of verbal façades led him to make an erroneous diagnosis. He thought that there was something going wrong with the English language of his day. His essay on "Politics and the English Language" makes this perfectly clear. "Most people who bother with the matter at all," he wrote, "would admit that the English language is in a bad way, but it is generally assumed that we cannot by conscious action do anything about it." Orwell believed that something could and should be done about it; but what he proposed to do simply showed how shallow his thinking about language was, and how uncritically he swallowed the doctrine of plain representation. He inveighed against the "bad influence" of American usage and its "debasing effect." He condemned expressions which he considered to betray "slovenliness," "ugliness," "lack of precision," "meaninglessness" and "pretentious diction." One of his recommendations was to memorize the sentence "A not unblack dog was chasing a not unsmall rabbit across a not ungreen field." In short, he showed exactly the same prescriptivist attitudes towards language as can be found in most published guides to "correct" usage, or any representative selection of complaints to the BBC about the decline of contemporary "standards" of English. Orwell attacks, as one essay on him puts it, "most of the misuses of language that have become the favourites of indignant letter-writers of any persuasion."

It would be misguided to defend Orwell by trying to distinguish his progressive and radical approach to questions of usage from the conservative, reactionary inspiration of the majority of "indignant letter-writers." The plain fact is that Orwell's attitude was no more enlightened than theirs. Accusing one's political opponents of "perverting the English language" is a game that both right and left can play, as recent arguments about nuclear weapons and unilateral disarmament have all too clearly shown. The fact that in the view of many observers the left emerged victorious from that particular fracas should not be misinterpreted. Appeal to the doctrine of plain representation is a double-edged weapon. To those inclined to think otherwise I would recommend consideration of two 1983 examples where the concept of Newspeak is invoked under the banner of writers not notorious (*pace* Orwell) for their left-wing sympathies.

The first is provided by an article in the *Times* entitled "How Newspeak Leaves Us Naked" (February 1, 1983), in which Roger Scruton uses a criticism of the definitions provided by the Moscow Novosti Press Agency's *Short Guide to Political Terms* (which countenances "democracy" as genuine only when understood as preceded by the adjective "socialist" and definitionally underwritten by the "dictatorship of the proletariat") as a springboard for an attack upon feminism. Feminism is described as "an ideology which, like communism, seeks to abolish history, to abolish human nature, and to abolish every thought which conflicts with its dominant and erroneous idea—the idea of the moral indistinguishability of men and women." Feminism, the article continues, "seeks to appropriate not only vocabulary, but also grammar, and to eliminate gender from a language structured by gender distinctions." (This is presumably a reference to controversies about using the masculine pronoun as the unmarked anaphoric form in sentences like *No one ought to forget his linguistic obligations to the community*.)

My second example is Friedrich von Hayek's onslaught on the phrase *social justice* (the *Times*, November 11, 1983). Hayek endorses Charles Curran's condemnation of this expression as "a semantic fraud from the same stable as *People's Democracy*," and describes the adjective *social* as "probably the most confusing and misleading term of our whole political vocabulary." The villain of the piece is Rousseau, apparently, in whose *Contrat Social* the wretched term "appears as an essential part of the rhetorical substitute for conventional morals." *Social*, in short, is castigated by Hayek as a "weasel word"; and a weasel word is described as a word "used to draw the teeth from a concept which one is obliged to employ, but from which one wishes to eliminate all implications that challenge one's ideological premises." The reader might perhaps have more confidence in this description were it not that this condemnation appears under a caption which advertises "F. A. Hayek on Newspeak exemplified." Does that make *Newspeak* itself a weasel word? And if so, which word shall escape whipping? Logophobia is evidently not a disease confined to any particular segment of the political spectrum.

In case the juxtaposition of these two examples might tend to cause apoplexy in some readers, perhaps it is worth interjecting a disclaimer. There is, indeed, a distinction to be drawn between the political ranting of a Scruton and the political rationale of a Hayek. The point, however, is that both can use the doctrine of plain representation for their own purposes: and for every Scruton or Hayek there will be an Orwell or an Orwellian to complain about the other side's use of expressions like *pacification, nuclear deterrent* and *acceptable casualties.* Propaganda always lays claim to a linguistic monopoly of truth.

The real misrepresentations which are central to these arguments and counter-arguments are not abuses of the English language at all. They are much more fundamental. They are abuses of our concept of a language itself. The reason why there could be no such language as Orwell's Newspeak is identical with the reason why there could be no such language as the idealized Oldspeak to which it stands opposed. No language can ever give us "plain representation," and it is an intellectual deception to imply that we should expect it to. The doctrine of plain representation is simply linguistic utopianism. Like all forms of utopianism, it provides countless traps for the simple-minded and endless claptrap for charlatans to exploit.

As the real—rather than the fictional—1984 arrives, we find the English-speaking community in a comical-tragical state of legislative turmoil over questions of "plain language." On one side of the Atlantic, British farmers are not allowed to call fresh milk "fresh" when it has come straight from the cow. Why not? Paradoxically, *because* it has come straight from the cow. (It may, of course, become "fresh" two days later, having been pasteurized in the interim.) Meanwhile on the other side of the Atlantic, we find states all over America rushing in legislation to protect the common man against the complexities of Oldspeak. Such enactments require, for example, that "every consumer contract shall be written in a clear and coherent manner using words with common and everyday meanings." But over the rather crucial questions of which words actually have "common and everyday meanings" are, the plain-language legislators wisely draw the discreet semantic veil of silence.

For Orwell, it would doubtless be one of the ironies of history that the country which took the lead in "defending" its Vietnam policy externally by means of Newspeak should now take the lead in defending the rights of its own proletariat to use Oldspeak for internal domestic purposes. But the irony is not to be laid at history's door: it is a projection from Orwell's own misconceptions about the way linguistic communication works.

Calling a spade a spade is not something languages can do: only language-users. And if language-users do not like the word *spade*, or cannot make it mean what they want to, then they will make another, with or without government intervention. Orwell's classic series of mistakes was to suppose (1) that something called "the English language" lays down the true meaning of a word like *spade*; (2) that words like *spade* mean what they say; and (3) that anything which needs to be said can be said using words like *spade*—in short, by using words any ordinary man can understand because the words in question directly reflect a recognizable reality. This muddled complex of beliefs has become one of the most popular pieces of linguistic folklore of modern times. It was Orwell's naïve commitment to that folklore which led to his creation of the fictional antilanguage of Newspeak, and hence to his (deserved) canonization as a prophet of twentieth-century culture.

1984: Enigmas of Power

Irving Howe

It is a common experience to fear that the admirations of youth will wear thin, and precisely because *1984* had so enormous an impact when it originally came out more than thirty years ago, I hesitated for a long time before returning to it. I can still remember the turbulent feelings—the bottomless dismay, the sense of being undone—with which many people first read Orwell's book. My fear now was that it would seem a passing sensation of its moment or even, as some leftist critics have charged, a mere reflex of the cold war. But these fears were groundless. Having reread *1984*, I am convinced, more than ever, that it is a classic of our age.

Whether it is also a classic for the ages is another question. What people of the future will think about Orwell's book we cannot know, nor can we say what it might mean to those who will remember so little about the time of totalitarianism they will need an editor's gloss if they chance upon a copy. But for us, children of this century, the relation to *1984* must be intimate, troubled, nerve-wracking. In 1938 or 1939 the idea of a world divided among a few totalitarian superpowers, which Orwell made into the premise of his book, had not seemed at all farfetched. I remember hushed conversations about the possible shape of a world dominated by Hitler and Stalin, with perhaps a shrinking enclave of democracy in North America. Such nightmare-visions seemed entirely real during the years just before the war, and with sufficient reason. When Orwell published his book a decade later, in 1949, one felt that, despite his obvious wish to unnerve us with an

From *1984 Revisited: Totalitarianism in Our Century*. © 1983 by the Foundation for the Study of Independent Social Ideas. Harper & Row, 1983.

extreme version of the total state, he was presenting something all too familiar, even commonplace.

Also familiar, though in a somewhat different sense, was the body of detail about daily life in Oceania that Orwell built up. Many of the descriptive passages in *1984* were simply taken over, with a degree of stretching here and there, from Orwell's earlier books or from his life-long caustic observations of twentieth-century England. In a review for the *Times Literary Supplement*, Julian Symons keenly remarked that

> In some ways life [in the Oceania of *1984*] does not differ very much from the life we live now. The pannikin of pinkish-grey stew, the hunk of bread and cube of cheese, the mug of milkless Victory coffee with its saccharine tablet—that is the kind of meal we may very well remember; and the pleasures of recognition are roused, too, by the description of Victory gin (reserved for the privileged—the "proles" drink beer), which has "a sickly oily smell, as of Chinese rice-spirit," and gives to those who drink it "the sensation of being hit on the back of the head with a rubber club." We can generally view projections of the future with detachment because they seem to refer to people altogether unlike ourselves. By creating a world in which the "proles" still have their sentimental songs and their beer, and the privileged consume their Victory gin, Orwell involves us most skilfully and uncomfortably in his story.

Symons might have added that in Orwell's earlier writing he had already focused almost obsessively on the gritty discomforts of urban life, the bad smells, the sour tastes, the grimy streets, the filthy rooms, the sweat-stained bodies. As it turned out, the unfuture of Oceania had some pretty keen resemblances to the immediate past of England.

Resemblances, also, to the years of Stalinist terror in Russia. The grilling of Winston Smith by the Oceania authorities, the alternation between physical beatings and sympathetic conversations, the final terrifying appearance of O'Brien, master of power—all these recall or parallel Arthur Koestler's account in *Darkness at Noon* of how the NKVD interrogated its victims. Koestler's description, in turn, anticipated closely what we have since learned about the methods of the Soviet secret police. It was to Orwell's credit that he understood how the imagination flourishes when it is grounded in common reality.

He knew, as well, that to make credible the part of his book which would spiral into the extraordinary, he had first to provide it with a strong foundation of the ordinary. Or to put it another way, he knew that his main problem was to make plausible—which, one might remember, is not the same as the probable—his vision of how certain destructive tendencies of modern society could drive insanely forward, unbraked by sentiments of humaneness or prudence.

Yet while rereading *1984*, I have come to recognize still another way in which it all seems decidedly familiar—but *this* familiarity causes shock.

The very idea of a totally controlled society in which a self-perpetuating elite rules through terror and ideology no longer strikes us as either a dim horror or a projection of the paranoid mind. In the few decades since Orwell wrote, we have gone a long way toward domesticating the idea of the total state, indeed, to the point where it now seems just one among a number of options concerning the way men live. The thought that totalitarianism is a constant, even commonplace possibility in the history of our time—this may prove to be as terrifying as the prospect that we might sooner or later be living under an Orwellian regime. No sensible person could have taken *1984* as an actual prediction; even those who read the book with malice or loathing knew it had to be taken as a warning, no doubt a fearful warning. That in its fundamental conception it should now seem so familiar, so ordinary, so plausible, is—when you come to think of it—a deeply unnerving fact about the time in which we live. But a fact it is.

II

To ask what kind of book *1984* is may seem a strange, even pedantic question. After all, you might say, millions of people have read the book and appreciated it well enough without troubling their heads about fine points of genre. Yet the question is neither strange nor pedantic, since in my experience there remains among Orwell's readers a good portion of uncertainty and confusion about what he was trying to do. People will often say, "Look, we're getting close to the year 1984 and we aren't living in the kind of society Orwell summoned; doesn't that mean he was exaggerating or perhaps that he was morbid?" To this kind of complaint there is a simple enough answer: It's in the very nature of anti-utopian fiction to project a degree of exaggeration, since without exaggeration the work would be no more than still another realistic portrait of totalitarian society.

Other complaints, being more sophisticated, take on a "literary" edge. Some of them, still often heard, are that the book contains no "real characters," or that there isn't enough of a credible social setting, or that the psychological vision of the story is somewhat rudimentary. Such complaints have really to do with genres or misunderstandings of genres; they reflect a failure to grasp the kind of fiction Orwell was writing and what could legitimately be expected from it. When a critic like Raymond Williams says that *1984* lacks "a substantial society and correspondingly substantial persons," he is (almost willfully, one suspects) missing the point. For the very premise of anti-utopian fiction is that it sketch an "inconceivable" world in such a way as to force us, provisionally, to credit its conceivability; that it project a world in which categories like "substantial society . . . substantial persons" have largely been suppressed or rendered obsolete. In actuality a society like that of Oceania may be impossible to realize, but that is not at issue here. A writer may, in the kind of fiction Orwell was composing, draw the shadows of "the impossible" as if they were real possibilities—if only in order to persuade us that finally they are not possible. As it happens, we have come close enough during the last half century to a society like Oceania for the prospect of its realization to be within reach of the imagination. And that is all a writer of fiction needs.

There are kinds of fictions that should not really be called novels at all: think of Voltaire's *Candide*, Swift's *Gulliver's Travels*, Peacock's *Crotchet Castle*. In *Anatomy of Criticism*, Northrop Frye, hoping (probably in vain) to check the modern tendency to lump all fictions as novels, describes a kind of fiction he calls Menippean satire, "allegedly invented by a Greek cynic named Menippus." This fiction "deals less with people as such than with mental attitudes . . . and differs from the novel in its characterization, which is stylized rather than naturalistic."

A quarter of a century ago, when first writing about *1984*, I thought this a satisfactory description of the kind of book Orwell had composed; but now I would like to modify that opinion. Almost everyone has recognized how brilliant Orwell was in finding symbolic vehicles and dramatic instances through which to render the "mental attitudes" about which Frye speaks. Think only of Newspeak and Big Brother, Hate Week and memory hole, all of which have entered our speech and consciousness as vivid figures. (A few years ago I visited a Canadian university where the wicked students had baptized a new campus building—vast, windowless, cement-ugly—as the Ministry of Love; and so, I am certain, it will be called for decades to come.) There remains, then, good reason to see *1984* as an instance of "Menippean satire"—but only in part.

For in going back to the book, I have learned to appreciate parts that now strike me as novelistic in the usual sense. Especially those parts in which Winston Smith and Julia try to find for themselves a patch, a corner where they can be alone and make love. Here bits of individuality begin to make themselves felt: Julia's boldness, for instance, in arranging their escapade to the country, where they can be free of the hated telescreen, or her charming indifference to all ideologies, as when she falls asleep during Winston's excited reading from the forbidden book, Emmanuel Goldstein's *Theory and Practice of Oligarchical Collectivism.*

I now think that *1984* ought to be read as a mixture of genres, mostly Menippean satire and conventional novel, but also bits of tract and a few touches of transposed romance. Such a description may be helpful, although not because anyone is foolish enough to want exact categories; it may train us, at the least, to avoid false expectations when we read.

III

An anti-utopian fiction must have a touch or two of excess. There has to be a story which takes the familiar conventions of the once-fashionable utopian novel and stands them on their heads. Elsewhere I've described that touch of excess as "the dramatic strategy and narrative psychology of 'one more step' . . . one step beyond our known reality—not so much a picture of modern totalitarianism as an extension, by just one and no more than one step, of the essential pattern of the total state." But this excess can of course consist of more than one step; it might be two or three, yet not many more steps than two or three, since then the link of credence between writer and reader might be broken by a piling on of improbabilities.

What has especially struck me in rereading *1984* is that, yes, it's true that in an anti-utopian fiction the writer can afford at most a few steps beyond our known reality, but he is likely to achieve his strongest effects precisely at the moment when the balance teeters between minimal credence and plummeting disbelief. For at such a moment we ask ourselves: Can things *really* go this far? And it is then that our deepest anxieties are aroused. Is it conceivable that the total state could be so "total," could break and transform human beings so far beyond what "human nature" may be expected to endure? We think and hope not, but we cannot be certain. We know that the total state has already done things earlier generations would have supposed to be impossible.

One such moment occurs in *1984* when Orwell turns to sexuality in Oceania. Members of the Outer Party—we remain in the dark about the Inner Party—are shown to be trained systematically to minimize and deny the sexual instinct, certainly to separate the act of intercourse from sensual pleasure or imaginative play. There can be no "free space" in the lives of the Outer Party faithful, nothing that remains beyond the command of the state.

Sexual energy is to be transformed into political violence and personal hysteria. The proles are permitted to drift into promiscuity, their very sloth and sleaziness a seeming guarantee against rebellion, but members of the Outer Party caught in promiscuous relations with one another face the most stringent penalties.

About all this Orwell is very careful:

> The aim of the Party was not merely to prevent men and women from forming loyalties which it might not be able to control. Its real, undeclared purpose was to remove all pleasure from the sexual act. Not love so much as eroticism was the enemy, inside marriage as well as outside. . . . Sexual intercourse was to be looked upon as a slightly disgusting minor operation. . . . The Party was trying to kill the sex instinct or, if it could not be killed, then to distort and dirty it.

It remains a fascinating question whether Orwell had captured here an essential part of the totalitarian outlook or had gone too far beyond "one more step." We know that in the years of Stalinism the Soviet Union favored, at least publicly, a prudish, sometimes a repressive antisexuality. But there is no evidence that during those years—and this is the period upon which Orwell drew for his book—Communist Party members were forced to suffer greater sexual repressiveness than the rest of the population. If the evidence is skimpy, Orwell was nonetheless touching on something very important here; he was taking an imaginative leap from totalitarian "first principles" concerning, not so much sex, certainly not sex in its own right but the threat of "free space," that margin of personal autonomy which even in the worst moments of Stalinism and Hitlerism some people still wanted to protect. And it was this margin that Orwell took to be the single great "flaw" of all previous efforts to realize the totalitarian vision. Whether a complete or "total" totalitarianism is possible, or possible for any length of time, is not, I want to repeat, the question. All that matters, for our purposes, is that it be plausible enough to allow a fictional representation.

Winston Smith's journey from rebellion to breakdown is a doomed effort to recover the idea, perhaps even more than the experience, of a personal self; to regain the possibility of individual psychology and the memory of free introspection. And this occurs in *1984*—I think it is one of Orwell's greatest strokes—not so much through ratiocination as through an encounter between two bodies. When Winston Smith and Julia make their first escapade out of London, carefully finding a patch in the woods where they can make love, they are not "in love," at least not yet. What happens between them is only—only!—the meeting of two eager bodies, animal-like if you must, but wonderfully urgent, alive, and good. They are free from the grip of the Party: this moment is theirs.

In this and a few other sections Orwell writes with a kind of grieving, muted lyricism, a hoarse lyricism which is about as much as, under the circumstances, he can allow himself. I have found myself moved, far more than when I first read the book, by these brief and unabashed celebrations of the body. A little freer in our language than in 1949, we would now say that Julia is a woman who likes to fuck, and it seems important to put it exactly that way, since in the wretched precincts of Oceania just about the best that anyone can do is fucking.

IV

Bolder still than Orwell's strategy of "one more step" in treating sexuality is his treatment of power. He tends to see the lust for power as a root experience, something that need not or cannot be explained in terms other than itself, and here too, I think, the passage of time has largely confirmed his intuitions. Let me draw upon your patience for a minute as I recall certain criticisms made by admiring critics of Orwell soon after *1984* came out. Philip Rahv, in a fine essay-review of the book, said that in one respect Orwell may have surpassed even Dostoevsky in grasping "the dialectic of power." *The Brothers Karamazov* shows the Grand Inquisitor as a tyrant ruling from benevolent intent: he believes man to be a weak creature, who needs the lash for his own good and can be happy only when the burden of freedom is lifted from his back. During the interrogation conducted by O'Brien, Winston Smith, hoping to please his tormentor, repeats the Grand Inquisitor's rationale for the holding of power:

> that the Party did not seek power for its own ends, but only for the good of the majority. That it sought power because men in the mass were frail, cowardly creatures who could not endure liberty or face the truth. . . . That the choice for mankind lay between freedom and happiness, and that, for the great bulk of mankind, happiness was better. That the Party was the eternal guardian of the weak, a dedicated sect doing evil that good might come, sacrificing its own happiness to that of others.

All of this strikes O'Brien as mere cant; he scorns it as "stupid." Turning up the dial of the machine that regulates Winston Smith's pain, he chastises him in these memorable words:

> The Party seeks power entirely for its own sake. We are not interested in the good of others; we are interested solely in power. . . . One does not establish a dictatorship in order to safeguard a revolution; one makes the revolution in order to establish the dictatorship. The object of persecution is persecution. The object of torture is torture. The object of power is power. . . .
>
> . . . Power is in inflicting pain and humiliation. Power is in tearing human minds to pieces and putting them together again in new shapes of your own choosing.

This exchange forms a key passage in *1984*, perhaps in the entirety of modern political discourse. Commenting on it in *Partisan Review* Philip Rahv offered a criticism in 1949 that seemed to me at the time both shrewd and valid:

> There is one aspect of the psychology of power in which Dostoevsky's insight strikes me as being more viable than Orwell's strict realism. It seems to me that Orwell fails to distinguish, in the behavior of O'Brien, between psychological and objective truth. Undoubtedly it is O'Brien, rather than Dostoevsky's Grand Inquisitor, who reveals the real nature of total power; yet that does not settle the·question of O'Brien's personal psychology, that is, of his ability to live with this naked truth as his sole support; nor is it conceivable that the party elite to which he belongs could live with this truth for very long. Evil, far more than good, is in need of the pseudo-religious justifications so readily provided by the ideologies of world-salvation and compulsory happiness. . . . Power is its own end, to be sure, but even the Grand Inquisitors are compelled . . . to believe in the fiction that their power is a means to some other end, gratifyingly noble and supernal.

Several decades have passed since Rahv wrote these trenchant lines and most of what has since happened gives one reason to doubt that he was entirely correct. Orwell was writing at a time when Stalin was alive and Hitler only recently dead: totalitarianism seemed an overpowering force, perhaps on the verge of taking Europe. The ideological fanaticism which a few years later would strike Hannah Arendt as one of the two underpinnings of the total state was still strong. For while it is true that Hitler and Stalin ruled through terror, it is also true that there were millions of people who took the Nazi and Communist ideologies, myths, and slogans with the utmost seriousness, yielding to them a devotion far more intense than traditional religions have been able to elicit in this century. Power may indeed be the beginning and the end of Party rule in Oceania, but at least in 1949 and for some years afterward it seemed hard to believe that an O'Brien would or could speak as openly as Orwell had him do, even to a victim he was soon to break.

Can we now be so certain that Orwell was wrong in giving Orwell that speech about power? I think not. For we have lived to witness a remarkable development of the Communist state: its ideology has decayed, far fewer people give credence to its claims than in the past, yet its power remains virtually unchecked. True, there is a less open use of terror, but the power of the state — a sort of terror-in-reserve — remains a total power. As lethargy and sloth overtake the Communist societies, it begins to seem that ideology will become among them a kind of fossilized body of tiresome and half-forgotten slogans. Not many educated Russians, including those highly placed within the party, can be supposed still to "believe" they are building the Communist society first expounded by Marx and Lenin. But the party remains.

What then do the apparatchiks believe in? They believe in their apparatus. They believe in the party. They believe in the power these enable. That a high Soviet bureaucrat might now talk to an imprisoned dissident in the bluntly cynical style that O'Brien employs in talking to Winston Smith does not therefore seem inconceivable. It does not even seem farfetched. The bureaucrat, especially if he is intelligent and has some pretensions to being sophisticated, might like to show his victim that he knows perfectly well that the totalitarian ethos has begun to decay, indeed, has entered a phase of transparency in which its cloak of the ideal has been stripped away. Now, this bureaucrat might not be as lucid as O'Brien, but he could easily speak to his victim as if to say, "Look here, my good fellow, I don't want to make a fool of myself with all that big talk about the 'classless society,' I simply want you to recognize, for your own good, who has the power and who intends to keep it."

I take it as a sign of Orwell's intuitive gifts that he should have foreseen this historical moment when belief in the total state is crumbling while its power survives. Whether such a condition signifies an explosive crisis or a period of low-keyed stability, we do not yet know. But there is now at least some ground for lending credence to Orwell's admittedly extreme notion that the rulers of the total state no longer need trouble to delude themselves, perhaps because they no longer can, about their motives and claims. The grim possibility is that they now have a realistic view of themselves as creatures holding power simply for the sake of power, and that they find this quite sufficient.

V

The most problematic, but also interesting, aspect of *1984* is Orwell's treatment of the proles.

> They were governed by private loyalties which they did not question. What mattered were individual relationships, and a completely helpless gesture, an embrace, a tear, a word spoken to a dying man, could have value in itself. The proles, it suddenly occurred to [Winston Smith] . . . were not loyal to a party or a country or an idea, they were loyal to one another.

With its echo of E. M. Forster, this is very touching, and it becomes more than touching when Winston looks for some agency or lever of rebellion that might threaten the power of the Party. "*If there is hope,*" he writes in his notebook, "*it lies in the proles.*" If . . . and then the paradox that even in the half-forgotten era of capitalism used to bedevil Socialists: "*Until they [the proles] become conscious they will never rebel, and until after they have rebelled they cannot become conscious.*" Orwell knew of course that traditionally Marxists had offered a "dialectical" resolution of this dilemma: the imperatives of action stir people into consciousness, and the stimulants of consciousness enable further action. A powerful formula, and millions of people have repeated it; but like other left-wing intellectuals of his day, he had come to feel dubious about its accuracy or usefulness. In writing *1984*, however, Orwell was wise enough to leave slightly open the question of whether the proles could exert a decisive power in modern society.

Here, if anywhere, Orwell made his one major error. The proles are allowed more privacy than Party members, the telescreen does not bawl instructions at them, and the secret police seldom troubles them, except occasionally to wipe out a talented or independent prole. What this must mean is that the Inner Party judges the proles to be completely crushed and tamed, no threat to its power either now or in the future, quite demoralized as individuals and helpless as a social class.

But the evidence of history—which ought, after all, to be crucial for a writer of an anti-utopian fiction—comes down strongly against Orwell's vision of the future. Europe this past half century has been convulsed by repeated, if unsuccessful, rebellions in which the workers (or proles) have played a major role, from East Berlin in 1956 to France in 1968, from the Hungarian Revolution to the rise of Solidarity in Poland.

But let us agree, for the sake of the argument, to move past the historical actuality or probability since, after all, it's always possible to read the evidence in conflicting ways. Suppose, instead, we focus only on the criterion of imaginative plausibility in forming a judgment about Orwell's treatment of the proles. Even then, I think, our sense of credence must be strained excessively. Let me take the liberty of quoting a few sentences from *Decline of the New* that I wrote soon after *1984* came out, because I think they are still pertinent:

> Orwell's treatment of the proles can be questioned on . . . fundamental grounds. The totalitarian state can afford no luxury, allow no exception; it cannot tolerate the existence of any group beyond the perimeter of its control; it can never become so secure as to lapse into indifference. Scouring every corner of society for rebels it knows do not exist [yet they might, they could!], the totalitarian state cannot come to rest for any prolonged period of time. To do so would be to risk disintegration. It must always tend toward a condition of self-agitation, shaking and reshaking its members. . . . And since, as Winston Smith concludes, the proles remain one of the few possible sources of revolt, it can hardly seem plausible that Oceania would permit them even the relative freedom Orwell describes.

If the "ruling circles" of Poland, Czechoslovakia, and Hungary could talk in private to O'Brien, they would tell him that, lucid as he may be on the subject of power, he may well be making a mistake in his view of the proles.

VI

An aura of gloom hangs over *1984*: the book ends with a broken Winston Smith drinking Victory Gin and blubbering his drunken love for Big Brother. He has made his "adjustment."

"*If there is any hope, it lies in the proles,*" Winston Smith had said. But is there any hope? That is not a question Orwell is obliged to answer; he need only ask it, with sufficient honesty and the despair that shows him to be a man of his century. The gloom that hovers over the book has been "explained" by some critics as a symptom of the grave illness Orwell was suffering at the end of his life, at the very time he wrote *1984*. Perhaps there is a small measure of truth in this, but basically it seems to me a rather stupid idea. A merely sick or depressed man could not have written with the surging inventiveness that shapes *1984*—and, in any case, where have these critics kept themselves this past half century? Haven't they heard the bad news? No, the gloom of *1984* is real and justified; but it is an energizing and passionate gloom.

If the extremism of Orwell's vision derives from a close responsiveness to the idea of a world in which human life is shorn of dynamic possibilities, it also reflects his growing distaste for politics itself, at least a politics that leaves no margin for anything but itself. And this may also account for the streak of conservatism in Orwell's outlook—a conservatism less of politics than of sensibility: that is, an appreciation for the way people actually live, the strengths of received ties and feelings. One of the most affecting parts of *1984* is Winston Smith's recurrent effort to recall fragments of the past, the days before the Party took power. He tries to remember how his mother caressed him as a child, simply because he was her child; he tries to summon the appearance of a destroyed church; he tries to put together an old rhyme, trivial in itself but rich with associations:

> Oranges and lemons, say the bells of St. Clement's,
> You owe me three farthings, say the bells of St. Martin's,
> When will you pay me? say the bells of Old Bailey?
> When I grow rich, say the bells of Shoreditch.

This conservatism of feeling, already present in Orwell's earlier books, is taken by some readers to conflict with his democratic socialist convictions. That would be true only if socialism were seen—as indeed both authoritarian left and reactionary right see it—as a total expurgation of the past, an attempt by a bureaucratic elite to impose "utopia" through terror. Orwell understood, however, that democratic socialism is an effort to extend what is valid in the past, to enlarge our freedoms and deepen our culture. The conservative sentiments Orwell reveals in *1984* not only aren't in conflict with his socialist opinions, they can be seen as sustaining them. Or so, at least, one hopes.

While writing this essay I have been asked several times by an editor of an American magazine eager for a quick word: "If Orwell were still alive, would he have remained a socialist?" The question is absurd on the face of it, since no one can possibly know. But this much can be said: Within his generation of left-wing writers and intellectuals, some have turned to the right, some have tried to refine their socialist values toward a greater stress on democracy, and others have abandoned their interest in politics entirely.

Which of these directions Orwell might have taken it would be foolish to say, except that it's hard to imagine him dropping his interest in politics entirely.

We do know that Orwell publicly repudiated efforts to use *1984* as a piece of antisocialist propaganda. A letter he wrote to an American correspondent puts his opinion with characteristic bluntness and lucidity:

> My recent novel [*1984*] is NOT intended as an attack on socialism or on the British Labour Party (of which I am a supporter) but as a show-up of the perversions to which a centralized economy is liable and which have already been realized in Communism and Fascism. I do not believe that the kind of society I describe *necessarily* will arrive, but I believe (allowing of course for the fact that the book is a satire) that something resembling it *could* arrive.

This is simply Orwell's opinion, and we know that writers often don't grasp the full implications of their work. It is quite possible, therefore, for some readers to say that while Orwell did not intend his book to be an attack on the socialist idea, it can be read that way.

And so it can. The vision of things Orwell presents need not necessarily lead to any one political conclusion, except a stress upon the urgency of democratic norms. Liberals, conservatives, and socialists can all argue from Orwell's text in behalf of their views, though the more sophisticated among them will recognize that a political position must be justified in its own terms, independently of any literary text.

Orwell understood that there is a profound tendency within modern society toward economic collectivism; that this tendency can take on a wide range of political colorations, from authoritarian to democratic; and that it can be deflected or modulated but probably cannot simply be annulled. The interpenetration of state and society, government and economy is simply a fact of modern life, quite as industrialization and urbanization have been. In correspondence from 1940, Orwell wrote, "There is [little] question of avoiding collectivism. The only question is whether it is to be founded on willing cooperation or on the machine gun"—that is, whether it will be democratic or authoritarian. This puts the matter with admirable precision. *1984* shows us what might happen if "the machine gun" triumphs; but the other choice remains to us.

"It Makes No Difference": A Utopia of Simulation and Transparency

Vita Fortunati

THE AMBIGUITY OF UTOPIA: UTOPIA AS GAME

Utopian literature is remarkable in being made up of a series of works linked by a tight network of echoes. The paradigm has its own rules and conventions to which all creators of successive utopias refer, to which, indeed, they must refer if they wish to create a utopia. Thus, in order to understand the significance of Orwell's anti-utopia, we must go back to the utopian tradition, for *1984* echoes this tradition. Orwell is mounting a concentric attack not only on the utopian tradition but also on the very structure of a utopia. Orwell's anti-utopia is not a work which lies outside the universe of utopia but both stems from and remains constitutionally within the framework of utopia. In this sense we may see how *1984* marks the end of utopia, or at least, of the possibility of utopia.

We must return first, for a moment, to the archetype of the genre, Thomas More's *Utopia*. Utopia, or the invention of a utopia, is a game based on the possibilities which experience offers, it is an *if* which is explored in all its possibilities. A utopia is not reality, but it is a *possible reality*. The game of utopia, like the game of chess, requires a set of pieces which have to obey certain rules. In order to be complete and well-ordered, the game must impose certain rules on time and space; the *ou-topos* has its own time and space. In the game of chess, the bishop, knight, rook, and queen simulate a

From *Orwell: Il Testo*, edited by Luigi Russo. © 1985 by Vita Fortunati. Aesthetica Edizioni, Palermo, 1985.

battle; in a utopia, the elsewhere, the journey, the arrangement of a city simulate society.

From the very beginning of the genre, utopia has had a ludic quality in that it is a speculative game with reality expressed in terms of a *political proposal* which is set up against reality. *The model suggests a possible reality which could substitute for the existing reality.* A utopia always maintains a close and specific relationship with the sociopolitical environment from which it stems. The alternative proposal which it represents in the form of a radically different society springs from a harsh criticism of the utopian writer's present reality of departure. The essence of utopia is to be found precisely in this shifting of position between a projected environment which is not reality and the actual reality to which the projected environment is in opposition. Utopia is thus a game played between the two poles of reality and fiction. Both the strength and the weakness of utopia rest in the basic underlying ambiguity of the genre. It is a strength in that a utopia represents a tension towards the elsewhere which reveals the ability to *think about the Other*, to go beyond the given facts and reality. It is a weakness because in utopia, in the model, there is the abstraction of the real and its *simplification*.

We have proposed the image of utopia as a game, but we must remember that every match of utopia versus reality reveals different characteristics from those of the preceding bouts since not only is any expression of utopia situated within a complex network of echoes of the preceding utopias, but it also sets up a specific relationship with the present which generates it. Each utopia is characterized by its identity with previous utopias and is distinguished by its diversity from these; thus the tradition of utopia is multiple and multifaceted. The march of utopias is a march of identical elements which are specific in their individual diversity.

Let us turn now to Orwell. In what sense may we speak of *1984* as the end of utopia? Why does Orwell annul the dialectical tension between the two elements which make up the essence of utopia, the tension, that is, between *what is and what should be, between reality and fiction*? In Orwell's work we find the total identification of the model with the reality, there is no longer any difference or distance between them. Everything is utopia, everything is project and fiction, contrast is lost. The projected reality has engulfed and entirely swallowed up reality. Thus utopia is no longer possible because the referent no longer exists and in its place there is the *simulacrum*. The connection with historical reality no longer exists, the possible project exists and is moved by a single energy source, *Power*. It is power which no longer has as its "telos" the organization of society but which is now simply an end in itself, a game played purely for its own sake. History no longer exists, history is a succession of simulacri, a *hyper-history*. It is a series of games with reality; paradoxically utopia has won because here *utopia finds its final realization*. An end has been made of the long cavalcade of utopias, the long series of proposals of possible worlds; the projects have been realized. Utopia thus becomes the re-creation of reality, the end of History. In Oceania, history is rewritten, re-created. "All history was a palimpsest, scraped clean and reinscribed exactly as often as was necessary."

The game may now be played *ad infinitum*, the projectualization of possible worlds now has no limits for the real referent has been removed. In Oceania, the Party suppresses all trace of its own historical origins in order to defend the legitimacy of the *perpetual present*, that is, of its own power. "Who controls the past controls the future: who controls the present controls the past."

I shall now attempt to consider the following points in an interpretation of Orwell's novel through a careful analysis of the text: 1) *1984* as the end of utopia; 2) *1984* as utopia as simulation; 3) *1984* as beyond the panoptic utopia; 4) *1984* as utopia as no-difference; 5) *1984* as parody of earlier utopias.

1984 AS THE END OF UTOPIA

At the level of narrative structure, the distinction between reality and fiction, between the world of the reader and the place of the utopia, has been removed in *1984*. In earlier literary utopias the dislocation was achieved through the journey. The journey emphasized the detachment from the departure reality for the two worlds existed in two different spaces, the utopia was clearly situated in an *elsewhere*, the time and space coordinates of which, however, remained intentionally imprecise. In Orwell's utopia, as in Zamyatin's *We*, which stands as the primary twentieth-century anti-utopia model, the journey has been eliminated and the dislocation is now not spatial but temporal.

When Orwell's novel was first published, the title "*1984*" had the metaphorical function of alluding to a time in the future which was, however, not too distant from the present of the reader. It is interesting to note how the temporal dislocation around which the book is constructed is still effective even today when we have actually reached and indeed passed the year 1984. In my interpretation, this is because the figurative strategies used within the text create an effect of total ambiguity. The ambiguity stems from the difficulty of drawing a clear distinction between dream and reality, between the subjective world and the objective world. The entire third section of the novel is characterized by this blurring of limits. Winston

Smith does not know where he is, he cannot tell day from night. He no longer has a sense of time and space. The atmosphere is that of a terrible nightmare dominated by ominous deformed images of animals like frogs and rats and by expressionistic visions of huge women of Swiftian proportions "with great tumbling breasts," of skull-like faces and by repulsive smells of vomit, sweat, reeking breath. Winston Smith lives in a state of lethargy or semiconscious stupor: "He had the impression of swimming up into this room from some quite different world, a sort of underwater world far beneath it." "He moved himself mentally from place to place, and tried to determine by the feeling of his body whether he was perched high in the air or buried deep underground."

Several critics have observed that the opening sentence of the novel, "It was a bright cold day in April, and the clocks were striking thirteen," is a superb example of the technique of defamiliarization [*ostranenie*], the kind of writing that transmits to the reader a shiver of worrying strangeness and unfamiliarity. Oceania is a world half-familiar and half-fantastic, where fantastic is understood in the sense of uncanny. While on the one hand the sentence recalls the conventions of English poetic tradition from Chaucer to Eliot, it nonetheless simultaneously turns these upside down by introducing transgressive elements which do not belong. The phrase "the clocks were striking thirteen" is a violation of the standard code for telling the time in Western society. In Oceania, April is not "wet" as both poetic and folk tradition would have it but "bright and cold." The text abounds with examples like this, examples which bear witness to the elaborate figurative strategy which Orwell uses to distance the reader from empirical facts and push him or her towards a transgressive reading of the rhetoric of the text.

In *1984*, we have lost the clear-cut distinction between the two character-types of literary utopias, the *traveller*, who carries the values of the society of departure, and the *guide*, who is the character within the utopia who expounds the principles on which the utopia world in question is based. Winston Smith, a citizen of Oceania, is ambiguously both inside and outside the utopia.

Orwell's camera moves in close-up or long shot to his characters depending on whether they express the function of the classical dupe of satirical tradition, who is blind to, or incapable of, perceiving the environment around him which he endures passively, or the external eye which can take in and also criticize the dystopic facets of Oceania civilization, thus rendering his relationship with the surrounding world problematical. From this point of view, Orwell brings into the utopia, which generally gives so little attention to individual differences and is utterly devoid of any psychological bent the traditional analysis of characters typical of the novel as literary form. Irving Howe is correct in stating that *1984* must be read as a text in which different genres are interwoven and interact: utopia, romance, satire, essay and standard novel.

The final interview between Winston Smith and O'Brien may be read not only as the rewriting, in terms of parody, of the scene of the Grand Inquisitor, but also as the rewriting of the dialogues which typically appear in utopias. This dialogue no longer shows traces of the characteristic dialectical dialogue, expressing a polyphony of voices, but is in reality a simulated dialogue in which the two speakers do not reveal different points of view. Winston is not the carrier of an alternative reality, he is, as we shall see below, the other face of O'Brien, his double. Opposition is not possible in Oceania society. Winston Smith is O'Brien's accomplice in the gratuitous power game because he consciously agrees to take part in it.

1984 AS UTOPIA OF SIMULATION

Oceania is a huge simulacrum of Power, where the sense of the sign no longer connects with a referent. The continually repeated and multiplied images of the enormous face of Big Brother do not connect with anything material, but rather with a vacuum or an absence. Political acts have been reduced to simulated acts, Power has been stripped of its political dimension. The social scene in Oceania is an empty stage on which remain only the signs of a power emptied of all morality and moral principle. It is power which is the object of social demand for signs of power. Thus in Oceania, there are the massive rallies of "Two Minutes Hate" or the public spectacles of the hangings, where methods of mass communication are exploited just as they were in the great Nazi rallies so carefully orchestrated by Albert Speer, the inventor of the terrifying aesthetics of collective gatherings. As political morality no longer exists in Oceania, Power is forced to recreate it by means of the *fiction* of Conspiracy and Scandal. The game of Power is the spectacle which O'Brien has to create for himself, a game which can be infinitely repeated. As O'Brien says to Winston Smith: "This drama that I have played out with you during seven years will be played out over and over again generation after generation, always in subtler forms."

The Power game is a competitive game and in order to play it O'Brien has to train an opponent. It has to be a real opponent, one at his own level, for parity of the contenders is one of the rules of the game. It has to be for the final victory to be full, satisfying and pleasurable. The situation in Oceania is paradoxical, for in order to express itself Power requires resistance and an opponent. The total control which Power holds makes the Power game even more difficult and it is thus the simulation of the opposition which must be as plausible as is possible in terms of simulation. It is for this reason that the novel gives more space to the description of the preliminary preparation than to the ultimate match between O'Brien and Winston Smith.

The relationship between Winston Smith and O'Brien may thus be interpreted as a competitive game for power, a gratuitous game, a game which exists only for its own ends. Here we may again see a clear parody of the utopian ideal in which power is always instrumental.

> The Party seeks power entirely for its own sake. We are not interested in the good of others; we are interested solely in power. Not wealth or luxury or long life or happiness: only power, pure power. What pure power means you will understand presently. We are different from all the oligarchies of the past, in that we know what we are doing. . . . Power is not a means, it is an end.

It is Orwell himself who suggests this interpretation of the relationship between Winston Smith and O'Brien—the relationship between two players who have accepted the rules of the game—as a framework to the novel by alluding throughout the work to various types of game, which we may classify following Caillois' classification as "competition, simulacrum, chance and vertigo." In the final pages of the book, Orwell applies the game metaphor to society as a whole. Winston plays a single game of chess, but it is a game which is entirely simulated and manipulated, because Big Brother has already won, Big Brother always wins.

The game between Winston Smith and O'Brien is characterized by a highly charged emotional content. The two establish between themselves what amounts to a sadomasochistic relationship of victim and torturer. They operate within the same framework, for they share and accept the same rules of the game. From this point of view, the figure of Smith, which is generally accepted within Orwell criticism as that of the rebel, in my opinion needs to be rethought and reanalyzed. Winston Smith is far from being merely an innocent victim. He enters the game voluntarily and fully aware; he enters the game knowing that the Brotherhood cannot exist and is only an illusion. "What was happening was only the working-out of a process that had started years ago. . . . He had accepted it. The end was contained in the beginning." The match between Winston Smith and O'Brien can thus be seen as the initiation of Smith to pure power, during which he learns its rules, that is, the rules of the game, by playing it.

1984 MARKS THE TRIUMPH OF THE PANOPTIC SOCIETY WHILE SIMULTANEOUSLY GOING BEYOND IT

In Oceania, the telescreen rules everything and everyone; it becomes the principle of total visual control. The echoes of Bentham's utopia, the *Panopticon*, are inevitable and important.

The Panopticon took form as an architectural project in which the rationalization and the control of space became the exercise and history of Power. The Panopticon is the circular prison with the watchtower at the centre from which the guard can see the prisoners without being seen. Bentham applies the panoptic machine with rigorous thoroughness to all possible real-life uses, prisons, factories, hospitals, mental asylums, schools, wherever a number of people have to be watched over. From this point of view, then, Oceania is the panoptic society *par excellence*. The telescreen is the invisible eye which sees and controls everything. However, while it is true that Oceania represents the panoptic society *par excellence*, it is equally true that it nonetheless marks the end of such a society.

Just as the actual referent of the utopia project has been eliminated, so in the dialectical relationship of Controller–Controlled the telescreen is also a pure simulacrum. Behind the telescreen there is a vacuum and the medium projects the image of a controller who does not actually exist. Bentham's universe presupposed a hierarchical society in which there were well-defined roles and a dialectical relationship between those who watch and those who are watched.

Orwell reduces this tension between the Watcher and the Watched to nothing. In Oceania, everyone is watched. In place of the guard there is the telescreen, which is the medium through which the panoptic machine works. In this sense, Orwell goes beyond the panoptic society and presages the endemic widespread presence of television and the hidden power of the media, which destroy the distinction between active and passive. During the Two Minutes Hate there is a total, passive enjoyment of the simulation. The image and the model become more real than the real. The telescreen becomes a kind of parody of the religious metaphor of the omnipresent Eye of God which sees you at every moment. From being a metaphor which gave substance to a divine and moral principle, the eye has become a machine for social control.

1984 AS UTOPIA OF NO-DIFFERENCE

In the society which Orwell creates in *1984*, oppositional, binary, Saussurian logic no longer exists. As we have seen, there exits instead the logic of abstract models, uprooted from any actual reference to reality. In the universe of total simulation there governs a total relativity, which means manipulation and combination of models. Orwell's Newspeak marks the final death of oppositions and heightens the elimination of dialectic. Now thought is possible only as automatic thought, which does not develop but simply repeats in a stereotypical way the party slogans. Oceania is the world of no-difference, of the interchangeability of terms: war is peace and peace is war. It is a world in which positive and negative generate and replace one another in turn. "It does not matter whether the war is actually happening, and, since no decisive victory is possible, it does not matter whether the war is going well or badly." The phrase which recurs in an almost obsessive manner throughout the novel is "it (the Party) makes no difference," or, in an alternative form, "nothing makes a difference." This above all emphasizes the neutralizing and homogenizing character of Oceania society. The law of equivalence governs everything; it is a world in which dialectic has been eliminated and the sequence of contradiction, alternative and head-on clash is no longer possible. The Party cancels all traces of difference through the elimination of historical memory. Thus history is "vaporized." "And so it was with every class of recorded fact, great or small. Everything faded away into a shadow-world in which, finally, even the date of the year had become uncertain."

The fate of *1984* as a text seems to indicate that the "no-difference" of Oceania society is also the "*in*difference" of our own society, and that there is a close relationship between us as readers and *1984* as text. For it is a text which today, now that Orwell's year has come and gone, seems to run the risk of being safely filed away out of thought, of being defused of its worrying, ominous charge simply because we are afraid of being afraid. It is a text which, because of its very popularity, its widespread diffusion, and its notoriety, has tempted the fate, and continues to do so, of being tamed and rendered innocuous through familiarity. When we reread Orwell today, we must make the effort to reappropriate the horror which it describes and produces, for this is the very horror which our own society is surreptitiously administering to us daily in small but significant doses.

1984 AS A PARODY OF UTOPIA

In *1984*, Orwell takes the ideas and images with which the utopian imagination had worked in the past and turns them upside down. He makes the language of utopia his own and rewrites it in terms of parody. *1984* sets up an intertextual dialogue with the utopias which precede it and inverts the values of these models using characteristic techniques of parody such as amplification and grotesque.

It is not within the scope of this present study to analyze in detail the many parts of the novel where Orwell may be seen to be rewriting the utopias of the past. However, I shall here concentrate on two of three of the most important *topoi* of utopian literature which Orwell systematically inverts or turns inside out. In this way, the anti-utopia explodes the whole genre of utopia.

The typical utopian city, well-ordered, harmonious and perfect in all its parts, the very layout of which reflects the sociopolitical ideals of the utopian writer, in *1984* is represented by a decaying, bomb-shocked London of ruins and skull-like houses denuded of windows. In the standard utopia there ruled a harmonious relationship between both man and his environment and man and the State. The constant watchful regard of Power in Oceania does not unite its people, but rather isolates and separates them.

As O'Brien says, "It is the exact opposite of the stupid hedonistic Utopias that the old reformers imagined." It is thus in no way a utopia founded on love and justice. "A world of fear and treachery and torment, a world of trampling and being trampled upon. . . . The old civilizations claimed that they were founded on love or justice. Ours is founded upon hatred. In our world there will be no emotions except fear, rage, triumph, and self-abasement."

The total transparency of the standard utopian place which hides nothing of its workings and leaves no shadow of doubt or uncertainty of its motives and functions under the all-pervading light of rationality, honesty and truth becomes in Oceania total invisibility. In Oceania, mirrors do not reflect; glass is opaque. As C. S. Lewis said, a totally transparent world is an invisible world.

The appendix giving details of Newspeak may also be read as a sort of parody of the utopian principle that everything should be apparent at a single glance, including the language. With Newspeak, Orwell ridicules the various different attempts (for example, new alphabets) by earlier creators of utopias to invent a pure, simple language which would be transparent in all its parts. Newspeak is thus a parody of pure and simple language, a language mutilated and homogenized.

Even O'Brien the dictator may be seen as a parody of the creator of utopias, a moralist, censor, and pedagogue who wants to reform humanity, as represented in Winston Smith, "the last man" of a generation which is in the process of becoming extinct. O'Brien represents future humanity, the new man, man uprooted from his past culture and history, man with no memory, stripped of his own individual identity and his own past.

As a final point, given the importance with which Orwell invests his anti-utopia, I would like to examine the sections of the novel which deal with torture, the physical suffering of Winston Smith and his relationship with Julia.

These sections are generally seen as a further demonstration of the totalitarianism of Oceania or of any totalitarian utopia and as evidence of the persecution of the individual this entails, coupled with the impossibility of a private life within such a society. This is no doubt true, and Orwell wanted to underline this particular aspect in his work, yet I feel that a more satisfying and complete explanation may be found by considering these areas outside the context of certain aspects of the immediate postwar period and the cultural turmoil of the time in which the book was written.

It seems to me that even in these parts of the novel Orwell is stating his position with respect to the tradition of utopia. As far as the relationship between O'Brien and Winston Smith is concerned, Orwell repeatedly draws into evidence the sadomasochistic component present in the encounter, and in the torture chapter Winston Smith's corporeality is continually emphasized, with no attempt to hide the fact that his suffering is a brutally physical suffering. I would suggest that this is intended as a scorching reminder that points, paradoxically, to the overwhelming absence of such themes in earlier utopias. Utopia, and the whole tradition of utopias, may be seen as a vehicle for political statements. By choosing the literary form of the utopia, writers are able to bring into the open controversial areas of state organization such as the distribution of wealth and class relationships. In this sense, utopia has been a progressive influence, acting as the testing ground for alternative political proposals and the possibilities, both practical and theoretical, of imagining new aspects of the real situation. Orwell, however, has discovered the Achilles heel of the utopian exercise and in 1984 demonstrates that *Utopia* and its long chain of later imitations may be read as an operation of removal and exorcism of a very different series of difficult, controversial subjects which may be expressed simply as sex and crime.

More's Renaissance rationality, Bacon's proto-Illuminism, Bentham's Utilitarian rationality all reveal an effective phobia for all abnormal or deformed aspects of real life. It is not merely coincidence that the problems of sex, of women, and of crime are not present in any of the earlier utopias.

The anthropological model which underlies the utopian tradition is a model of rational perfectibility of both society and man, where reform of the State leads inevitably to the disappearance of all the dark or shadowy aspects of life. This model is shown to be insufficient and structurally unsound in Orwell's *1984*.

Orwell's conviction is that these shadowy aspects are not merely momentary blemishes on the history of mankind and that we must therefore come to terms with sexual tendencies and the physical nature of our bodies. Corporeality is exemplified through physical acts such as defecation and copulation. Swift and Bentham, to name only two of the more lucid creators of utopias, demonstrate a phobia about these aspects of real life which in the utopias of other writers, Fourier, for example, are on the other hand carefully compartmentalized and thus rendered innocuous. In *1984*, the horrendous torture scenes and Winston Smith's physical suffering as well as the debased relationship with Julia serve as a kind of moral blow. Orwell includes them as a sarcastic cry of rage against the systematic removal and ignoring of these aspects in previous utopias.

Finally, and to avoid the risk of being misunderstood, I would say that Orwell is forced to pay a certain price in his attempt to draw attention to and reverse this operation of systematic removal. Orwell has to homogenize the preceding utopias, and thus his reading of them annihilates the different meanings and values expressed in the heterogeneous collection of earlier expressions of the genre. Orwell is forced to place, at least implicitly, Communist, theocratic, right-wing and left-wing utopias on the same level. Orwell builds up an enemy with his own hands in order to shoot it down, creating the concept of utopia "tout court" without distinguishing one example from another in terms of merit or worth. This method cannot be approved from the point of view of methodology or history. His target thus is utopia understood as a totalitarian phenomenon, which finds its realization in a consolidation of homogeneity, of types, of repetitions and of orthodoxies. Once he has achieved this transformation, Orwell becomes extremely harsh in his criticism of such a phenomenon, yet it remains a criticism at the highest possible level, as he himself is the first to realize that the terms of the question have changed. The dominant element is now that of the mass society and of its totalitarian mentality: this is finally the society of no-difference, the transparent universe.

The high cost of Orwell's critical transformation of utopia is found in the loss of the highly charged tension of idealism, the missionary zeal and the tang of heresy which works of utopia express. Orwell's own criticism of utopia through *1984* should not be ignored and would seem to me to contradict certain instrumentalizations of his work which have been made and continue to be made.

We must see *1984* therefore as a lucid challenge flung to utopia by an intellectual who always liked to consider himself an "unwanted guerrilla." It is a challenge to utopia as a totalitarian phenomenon in the service of power, a challenge to the utopia which paralyzes the imagination by keeping it under utter control.

Chronology

1903	George Orwell (Eric Arthur Blair) born June 25 at Motihari, Bengal, to a middle-class English family which has been attached to the British colonial administration in India and Burma.
1917–21	After English preparatory schools, scholarship to Eton.
1922–27	Serves with Indian Imperial Police in Burma.
1928–29	In Paris, writes and works as dishwasher.
1930–34	Lives mainly in London. Publishes articles and translations.
1933	*Down and Out in Paris and London.*
1934	*Burmese Days* published in New York, for lack of an English publisher.
1935	*A Clergyman's Daughter.*
1936	*Keep the Aspidistra Flying.* Orwell marries Eileen O'Shaughnessy. Leaves for Spain in December to join anti-Fascists in Barcelona. Serves four months on the Aragon Front.
1937	*The Road to Wigan Pier.* Wounded in the throat, Orwell returns from Spain to England.
1938	*Homage to Catalonia.* After several months in sanatorium for treatment of tuberculosis, Orwell visits Morocco for winter.
1939	*Coming Up for Air.*
1940–43	*Inside the Whale.* Medically unfit for service, Orwell joins Home Guard. Writes and broadcasts for the BBC as wartime propagandist.
1943	Literary editor of the *Tribune*, a Labour Weekly.
1945	Correspondent for *The Observer.* Orwell's wife dies during surgery. *Animal Farm.*
1946	Rents house on Jura, in the Hebrides.
1947	Intermittent attacks of tuberculosis.
1949	*1984.* Marries Sonia Brownell. Enters sanatorium.
1950	Orwell dies in London, January 21.
1968	*Collected Essays, Journalism and Letters* published.

Contributors

HAROLD BLOOM, Sterling Professor of the Humanities at Yale University, is the author of *The Anxiety of Influence, Poetry and Repression*, and many other volumes of literary criticism. His forthcoming study, *Freud: Transference and Authority*, attempts a full-scale reading of all of Freud's major writings. A MacArthur Prize Fellow, he is general editor of five series of literary criticism published by Chelsea House.

RAYMOND WILLIAMS, Judith F. Wilson Professor of Drama at Cambridge University, is the most influential of British Marxist critics of literature. His books include *Culture and Society, The Long Revolution*, and *The Country and the City*.

PAUL ROAZEN is the author of *Erik H. Erikson: The Power and Limits of a Vision, Helene Deutsch: A Psychoanalyst's Life*, and the forthcoming *Freud and His Followers*.

ANTHONY BURGESS, novelist and critic, is the author of *A Clockwork Orange, Earthly Powers*, and the Enderby novels, among others. His criticism includes a study of D. H. Lawrence and two books on Joyce.

DAPHNE PATAI teaches in the Women's Studies Program and in the Department of Spanish and Portuguese at the University of Massachusetts in Amherst. She is the author of *The Orwell Mystique: A Study in Male Ideology* and *Myth and Ideology in Contemporary Brazilian Fiction*.

ROY HARRIS is Professor of General Linguistics at Oxford University. His books include *The Language Myth* and *Approaches to Language*.

IRVING HOWE is Distinguished Professor of English at Hunter College. His best-known book is *World of Our Fathers*. He is also known for his studies of Faulkner, Hardy, and Sherwood Anderson.

VITA FORTUNATI is Associate Professor of Modern Foreign Languages at the University of Bologna. Her books include studies of the dandy in English literature and of literary utopias.

Bibliography

Atkins, John. *George Orwell: A Literary Study.* London: John Calder, 1954.

Bloom, Harold, ed. *Modern Critical Views: George Orwell.* New Haven, Conn.: Chelsea House, 1987.

Brander, Laurence. *George Orwell.* Toronto: Longman, 1954.

Burgess, Anthony. *1985.* London: Hutchinson, 1978.

College Literature 11, no. 1 (Winter 1984). Special George Orwell issue.

Glicksburg, Charles I. "George Orwell and the Morality of Politics." In *The Literature of Commitment.* Lewisburg, Pa.: Bucknell University Press, 1976.

Gross, Miriam, ed. *The World of George Orwell.* New York: Simon & Schuster, 1972.

Harris, Harold J. "Orwell's Essays and *1984.*" *Twentieth Century Literature* 5, no. 4 (January 1959): 154–61.

Hollis, Christopher. *A Study of George Orwell: The Man and His Works.* Chicago: Regnery, 1956.

Howe, Irving. "Orwell: History as Nightmare." *American Scholar* 25 (Spring 1956): 193–207.

———. *Orwell's 1984: Text, Sources, Criticism.* New York: Harcourt, Brace & World, 1963.

———. *1984 Revisited.* New York: Harper & Row, 1983.

Hynes, Samuel, ed. *Twentieth Century Interpretations of 1984.* Englewood Cliffs, N.J.: Prentice-Hall, 1971.

Jensen, Ejner J., ed. *The Future of Nineteen Eighty-Four.* Ann Arbor: University of Michigan, 1984.

Kubal, David. "Freud, Orwell, and the Bourgeois Interior." *Yale Review* 67, no. 3 (March 1978): 389–403.

Kuppig, C. J., ed. *Nineteen Eighty-Four to 1984.* New York: Carroll & Graf, 1984.

Lief, Ruth Ann. *Homage to Oceania: The Prophetic Vision of George Orwell.* Columbus: Ohio State University Press, 1969.

Macdonald, Dwight. "Varieties of Political Experience." *New Yorker,* March 28, 1959, 132–47.

McNamara, James, and Dennis J. O'Keeffe. "Waiting for 1984." *Encounter* 59, no. 6 (December 1982): 43–48.

Modern Fiction Studies 21, no. 1 (Spring 1975). Special George Orwell issue.

Norris, Christopher. *Inside the Myth: Orwell: Views from the Left.* London: Lawrence & Wishart, 1984.

Rees, Richard. *George Orwell: Fugitive from the Camp of Victory.* London: Secker & Warburg, 1961.

Sandison, Alan. *The Last Man in Europe: An Essay on George Orwell.* London: Macmillan, 1974.

Stansky, Peter, and William Abrahams. *The Unknown Orwell.* New York: Knopf, 1972.

Trilling, Lionel. "Orwell on the Future." *New Yorker,* June 18, 1949, 78–83.

Vorhees, Richard J. *The Paradox of George Orwell.* Lafayette, Ind.: Purdue University Studies, 1961.

Walter, Nicolas. "George Orwell: An Accident in Society." *Anarchy* 8 (October 1961): 246–55.

Watt, Alan. "George Orwell and Yevgeny Zamyatin." *Quadrant* 28, nos. 7–8 (July–August 1984): 110–11.

Williams, Raymond. *George Orwell.* New York: Viking, 1971.

———, ed. *George Orwell: A Collection of Critical Essays.* Englewood Cliffs, N.J.: Prentice-Hall, 1974.

Woodcock, George. *The Crystal Spirit: A Study of George Orwell.* Boston: Little, Brown, 1966.

World Review 16 (June 1950). Special George Orwell issue.

Zwerdling, Alex. *Orwell and the Left.* New Haven: Yale University Press, 1974.

Acknowledgments

"George Orwell" by Raymond Williams from *Culture and Society 1780–1950* by Raymond Williams, © 1958 by Raymond Williams. Reprinted by permission of Columbia University Press.

"Orwell, Freud, and *1984*" by Paul Roazen from *Virginia Quarterly Review* 54, no. 4 (Autumn 1978), © 1977 by *Virginia Quarterly Review*. Reprinted by permission.

"Ingsoc Considered" by Anthony Burgess from *1985* by Anthony Burgess, © 1978 by Anthony Burgess. Reprinted by permission of Hutchinson & Co. (Publishers) Ltd.

"Gamesmanship and Androcentrism in *Nineteen Eighty-Four*" by Daphne Patai from *The Orwell Mystique* by Daphne Patai, © 1984 by Daphne Patai. Reprinted by permission of the author and the University of Massachusetts Press. The footnotes have been omitted.

"The Misunderstanding of Newspeak" by Roy Harris from *Times Literary Supplement* (January 6, 1984), © 1984 by *Times Literary Supplement*. Reprinted by permission.

"1984: Enigmas of Power" by Irving Howe from *1984 Revisited: Totalitarianism in Our Century* by Irving Howe, © 1983 by the Foundation for the Study of Independent Social Ideas. Reprinted by permission of Harper & Row Publishers.

"It Makes No Difference: A Utopia of Simulation and Transparency" (originally entitled "It Makes No Difference: *1984*, A Utopia of Simulation and Transparency") by Vita Fortunati from *Orwell: Il Testo*, edited by Luigi Russo, © 1985 by Vita Fortunati. Reprinted by permission of Professor Luigi Russo, Aesthetica Edizioni, Palermo, 1986.

Index